10/20

D0554033

The Evolving Church
and
The Sacrament of Penance

A Gift to
St. John Vianney Seminary

From the Jesuit Fathers of the
Missouri Province
Xavier Jesuit Center
Denver, Colorado
2004

Library of Congress Catalog Card Number: 78-65538

ISBN: 0-87193-072-2

Imprimi potest.
New York. July 10, 1978
Vincent M. Cooke, S.J., Provincial
New York Province of the Society of Jesus

Books published by the author:

Open to the Spirit: Religious Life after Vatican II

The Lord of Confusion

Probing the Spirit

Blessed Are Those Who Have Questions

TABLE OF CONTENTS

Introduction

The Origin of this Book; or, How Two Issues Became Intertwined

This book was born from the search for a good method to follow in discovering fitting structures and wise laws for the Church—an eminently practical preoccupation.

Soon it became clear that, to discover such a method, it was necessary to understand the evolving nature of the Church—a decisively theoretical task.

But, after all, such has always been the order of rational activity: practice must follow theory. Thus, we concluded that the foundational question of this book should be about theory: *What is the evolving Church?*

Once we have found a satisfactory answer to this question, we can look with greater confidence for that good method that will help us to discover fitting structures and wise laws.

To find out what the evolving Church is, we must wrestle with the issue of how to understand change in the Christian community. Change, however, does not take place in the abstract; it happens in the concrete world. Therefore, we must observe actual changes in the Church and then examine the causes that bring them about.

We looked for an ecclesial institution whose history would display such actual changes. There are many of these, of course. From among them, we have chosen the sacrament of penance, since it has undergone significant changes from the beginning to our own days. Reflection on it may lead us to conclusions concerning the whole community.

Hence, the other question of this book: *What is the evolving sacrament of penance?*

Admittedly, this is a broad issue. To handle it well, it will be necessary to break it down into smaller components such as: How did the sacrament of penance evolve? What are its structures today? At what point in its evolution has this institution arrived? What fitting structures and wise laws can we find to help it develop further?

We shall deal with these issues step by step.[1]

The Main Purpose of This Book

The main purpose of the book is the discovery of a good method. We work toward it from two directions, from the somewhat theoretical understanding of the nature of the evolving Church, and from the more practical observation of the evolution of structures and norms relating to the sacrament of penance.

Change has always caused problems in the Church; it still does. There are those who proclaim solemnly that what was good for past generations of Christians should be good enough for us; there are those who announce forcefully that the past should be forgotten and all things created anew. But, there is no method in such approaches. A living body such as the Church cannot be helped through simplistic slogans. Wisdom, divine and human, demands that the precise needs of the body should be assessed and

[1]This book focuses on changes, but, by implication, it deals constantly with permanency as well. The two are closely related to each other; one cannot be understood without the other. In many ways, the problem of our age is not only to understand change, but to understand the need for stability and continuity. Much that is in these pages shows precisely that.

whatever is necessary or useful for its further development should be given to it. It is not always easy to spot the real needs. A sensible method is needed to go about it.

If the method that we follow and propose (both!) proves itself useful, its application should not be restricted to finding fitting structures and wise laws for the sacrament of penance only; rather, it should be extended and applied far and wide. It could assist the process of the revision of the *Code of Canon Law,* in general; it could help with finding new norms for old institutions, in particular. By way of example, here are some of the particular questions of our times; good method could help to find the right answers:

> *What structures and laws do we need to keep the right balance between primacy and episcopacy?
> *What institutions and guidelines can we devise to sustain and increase the movement toward the unity of the Christian churches?
> *How can we find a better legal framework for Christian marriage?

And so forth. Who could enumerate all the problems that we have with our institutions?

If found, a good method can bring fruit a hundredfold —well beyond the immediate scope of this book.

The Structure of Our Five Questions

This book is built around five questions. For the sake of an easy overview, let us list them.

The first question is about historical events: how did the practice of reconciling sinners evolve? It refers to the sacrament of penance.

The second question is about ideas that inspired the evolution: how do ideas develop? It refers mainly to the evolving Church.

The third question is about persons who produce new ideas: how do persons change? It refers, again, to the evolving Church.

The fourth question is about the *New Rite of Penance* promulgated in 1973: what is the role of this document in an evolutionary process?

The fifth question is about ourselves and the future: how can we contribute to further evolution? It refers to both the evolving Church and the sacrament of penance. The two issues meet.

These are the five questions. There is one pattern of thought behind them. It consists of a heuristic structure bent on the discovery of the desired method.

(1) We begin by observing historical events. We ascertain that evolution has taken place. We do not write detailed history, but we indicate main trends that have led to clearly visible milestones. For our purpose, this much is required, and it is enough. Once the fact of evolution has been established, we can turn to the examination of its causes.

(2) To explain the flow of external events, we ask about the role of ideas behind them. More generally, we inquir ? about how ideas are born in any age, how they live on, and how they die. We search for criteria to determine which new insights are expressions of authentic Christian tradition and which ones are aberrations.

(3) New ideas are not born from thin air, they are produced by persons. Therefore, we reflect on the capacity of the person to change, to evolve, to develop. To un-

derstand this capacity is to move closer to the understanding of the evolving Church.

(4) We come to a fact again. In 1973 the *New Rite of Penance* was promulgated, an important milestone in the evolution of the sacrament. To determine its significance in an evolutionary movement, we use all the knowledge we gained in Chapters Two and Three about evolving ideas and developing persons.

(5) We gather together our discoveries and propose some fitting structures and new norms for granting pardon in the Church. Naturally enough, a distinction must be kept in mind: a course of action may be grounded in sound doctrine, it may be fitting pastorally, yet it may not be permitted by the present discipline. If such is the case, there are reasons to change the discipline.

This is the unifying pattern of thought behind our questions. Here is the method for all to see. Its rules are simple: if anyone wants to propose fitting structures and new norms for an ecclesiastical institution, he should be familiar with the development of that institution in history; he should understand how doctrine develops authentically; he should understand how persons grow in their capacity to know; he should be well acquainted with the present state of the institution, doctrinally and practically. If he has all that, the new structures that he proposes are likely to be fitting, the new norms wise, as they should be.

The Nature of the Book

The nature of this book is not simply to communicate knowledge to the reader, but to draw him into the process of our search, so that he can be with us also at the happy moment of discovery, if discovery is to be. Thus, we hope he will be more than a reader; he will be a partner in a common enterprise.[2]

Concerning Our Terminology

Due to the influence of classical Roman lawyers, and some modern philosophers as well, we are somewhat diffident toward definitions, especially at the beginning of an investigation . But, we hold that every person is able to build up an increasingly better understanding of the world, and of every object in it, as he progresses in knowledge. Thus, even if we do not give precise definitions at this point, we still feel that we must account for our understanding of some basic terms which are used repeatedly in this study.

There is the term *evolution*. We do not use it in a technical and biological sense. Rather, we mean by it a process of growth, of development, in a general sense. When we speak of the evolving Church, we mean the Christian community steadily progressing in wisdom and expanding in organization. If any doubt remains, the context should bring out the right meaning.

Our whole study is concerned with the *Church*, an analogous term if ever there was one. In general, it is true that we refer to the Roman Catholic Church. But, we should recall that there were no "Catholic" and "Orthodox"

[2]Following the pattern of this book, the reader himself could easily perform reflections similar to ours, on another topic. For example, he could gather the facts about the history of the Eucharist. He could, then, ask what ideas influenced the external changes; further, what evolution the persons themselves went through so that they were able to produce new ideas. He could, then, examine critically the state of our understanding of the Eucharist today, and what we can do to renew our celebrations.

churches before the Eastern schism, as there were no "Catholics" and "Protestants" before the Reformation.

We believe that our study has ecumenical dimensions, although they are more implicit than explicit. The method we propose for renewing structures and norms could serve the cause of unity better than some we have now. Also, a better understanding of the historical development of the Church can put into proper light, and reduce the significance of, the differences that caused the break between east and west, the reformers and the counter-reformers.

To speak of the *sacrament of penance* before the twelfth century may appear to be anachronistic, although many use that expression even when they refer to earlier times, not from ignorance but for the sake of easy communication. When it is important, we shall differentiate and use more historically correct language as the period warrants it. When it is not important, we, too, may use the expression "sacrament of penance" even for those times which preceded Peter the Lombard's classification and explanation of the seven efficacious signs; the reality was there even before it was scientifically recognized and classified. Again, the context should exclude any misunderstanding.

As a rule, we avoid the expression *sacrament of reconciliation* for penance in modern times because it is a misnomer. Today it would be better called "sacrament of forgiveness and healing." This name brings out the capacity of the sacrament to give life when it is lost, and healing when it is needed.

All other terms will be clarified, step by step, as the progress of our study warrants it.

Interdisciplinary Dimensions

This study is of an interdisciplinary character. It reaches out into the fields of theology, historical and systematic; it reflects on problems concerning Christian ethics; and, it searches for fitting structures and wise norms to be introduced by canon law.

For our purpose, such a unified approach is indispensable. There is only one sacrament of penance. Its existence is attested by Catholic dogma. Its meaning is explained further in systematic theology. There are moral obligations connected with it; the faithful must use it rightly, and the ministers must grant it responsibly. There are legal rights and duties attached to it to assure its ordered and peaceful use in the community. If the three aspects, dogma, moral and law are unduly separated, havoc follows. Unless someone knows what the sacrament is, he cannot understand the moral freedoms and obligations that it brings. Unless someone understands the moral issue, he cannot legislate about rights and duties in a balanced way.

Unfortunately, somewhere after the twelfth century, canon law became more independent from theology than was good for either of them; somewhere after the fifteenth century, theology itself suffered an all too sharp division between dogma and moral. Such divorces (because divorces they were: man put asunder what God had put together) had a disruptive effect on the life of the Church, and the effect is still with us—even after Vatican II.[3]

³Not even Vatican Council II remedied the situation. In schools of theology, to this day, the teaching of dogma is separated from that of Christian ethics, which in turn is separated from instruction in legal

Throughout our study, we uphold the unity that exists naturally between dogmatic beliefs, moral demands and legal norms. God's wholesome gifts should not be cut into parts that have no relation to each other; if such a disaster ever happens, their unity should be restored.

Nothing of what we have said, however, should be interpreted as being against legitimate methodological divisions among various branches of ecclesiastical sciences. Dogma, moral and canon law should each retain its peculiar character.

The Evolving Understanding of Sin and the Use of the Sacrament of Penance

In the Christian community, there was always a close relationship between the evolving understanding of sin and the use of the sacrament of penance. No wonder; penance was the medicine for the wound that sin inflicted on a person.

It follows, therefore, that to find fitting structures and wise laws for the sacrament of penance, it is necessary to take into account the undertanding of sin. By way of illustration, let us point to some historical situations.

In the early centuries, relatively few Christians went through the process of public penance. The reason was in the understanding of grievous sin. It was assumed that only relatively few were guilty to a degree that deserved or

---

norms. It is quite possible for a student to learn all about the dogma concerning the power of pardon, and to know little about the moral demands in using that power, and still less about the legal norms situating the sacrament in the community. When this happens, the student leaves the school with a deeply imbalanced knowledge, and innocent Christians will suffer at the hands of an ignorant minister. A pertinent comparison would be the student who graduates from medical school, his head full of theory about the beauty of the human body, but quite ignorant about diseases.

demanded public satisfaction. When such an event occurred, it was handled as a major issue that concerned the whole community.

In the Irish churches, private penance was of common occurrence; virtually all benefited from it. Such a new practice was possible only within a theoretical framework that expanded the scope of the rite of pardon: absolution could be granted by any priest to every sinner for all sins, great or small, and as many times as the sinner needed it.

The understanding of sin and the granting of pardon cannot be separated at any point of their history, past, present or future.

A Note on Our Third Question

Among all our questions, the third one may be the most important today. It goes to the heart of the matter. It raises the issue of interpreting history and the evolution of ideas in function of developing human persons. Obviously, our interest is not in biological or physical changes. It is in the development of a person's capacity to know. As the knower's ability to operate increases, knowledge expands and new things happen.

This problem is usually treated under the heading of "hermeneutics," a word that we use little. For the sake of clarity, we prefer to use the descriptive title, "development of persons."

The discovery that man's capacity to know determines, in several ways, the content and extent of his knowledge can help us significantly to understand the evolving Church. For a long time, the problem of the development of doctrine held the attention of theologians. Now, they are becoming increasingly aware that development is not confined to doctrine; it takes place in persons before it bears fruit in ideas.

A discovery of the obvious, someone might say. Why was it ever missed? We do not know—but, human beings have always been notoriously slow to notice the obvious, especially when it happens to be close to them.

At any rate, theologians are increasingly aware of the issue. As yet, the field of canon law has hardly been touched by it, but, in all cases where law must deal with human intentionality involving knowledge and ignorance, error and doubt, commitment or the lack of it, the benefit would be enormous. The key to the lasting reform of our marriage laws, in particular, may lie here.

The new knowledge that comes from the application of hermeneutical principles, or from the understanding of the development of human persons in their capacity to know, can help us explain many aspects of the life of the Church better than ever before. It can also enable us to define some future tasks with more competence and confidence than we had before. Here are some examples:

(1) There is the puzzling problem of the post-Vatican II years. The Council did so much to renew the Church, yet, in the years after it, we experienced so much fragmentation and disorientation; why? There is a new liturgy, more meaningful than the old, yet our churches are not filled; why? The Council tried to speak a contemporary language, yet the younger generations are not listening; why?

The answer to these questions is, obviously, complex. Many good things happened, and they should not be lost from sight. But, it is true that, on many points, there was a decline; why? Here is one explanation. As the Council ended, the Church at large was given new ideas representing the final stage of a development of doctrine that had taken place during the intense years of the Council. But, it was not realized that during the Council the bishops themselves changed. Their insights were given to the people who did not go through the same process, hence the response was often bewilderment, indifference, or quiet alienation. Structures can be changed overnight; new ideas can be spread with ease in a short time; therefore, a certain development of institutions, of doctrine, can seemingly be accomplished. But, as long as there is no new depth and breadth in the capacity of human persons to know and to love, there is no genuine progress.

(2) There is the issue of the reform of the laws of the Church. This is a monumental enterprise undertaken ever since 1963, when Pope John XXIII first appointed a commission for the revision of the *Code of Canon Law* of 1917. An immense amount has been written on various aspects of the reform, and virtually all these writings raise and answer the question of how the new law should be. Yet, the core of the problem is not there. It is, rather, how a canon lawyer should operate in the Church to come; how far his horizons should expand; how deeply he should be involved in the ongoing cultural development of every Christian community; what kind of legal categories he should use, or create whenever necessary. That is where the heart of the matter is. The primary task should be, then, to confront the issue of legal education in the Church. In the long run, the quality of the new laws will turn on the capacity of the lawyers. To confirm all this, legal history provides a striking example. Classical Roman law, with its delicate balances so well adjusted to the needs of the com-

munity, was developed by persons of increasingly broad intelligence, from most unpromising material, the strict laws of the Twelve Tables.

(3) There are difficult problems in missiology. A thinking person cannot help noticing a puzzling contrast between the pedagogy of God with his chosen people, the twelve Hebrew tribes, and the pedagogy of the Church with newly converted peoples. God imposed his demands on the Hebrews gradually. He had infinite patience with their slowness in grasping his words and putting his commandments into practice. He let their minds and hearts develop before he revealed to them the fulness of some of his teachings, before he exacted of them the demands of the new law. The Church imposes its demands right away, abruptly and in their totality, on all who ask for admission. It has little tolerance for gradual adaptation.

The Church may well be right; St. Paul was not very patient with pagan customs, either. But, if to live the Christian revelation means not only a readiness to say the Creed and a willingness to observe the commandments, but a genuine transformation of minds and hearts, then time should be allowed for such transformation. Should we pause and reflect on whether or not God's own pedagogy with his chosen people tells us something about how the Church should deal with newly converted peoples; whether for them, too, there should be a period of transition, necessary for slowly growing into the broad horizons of divine revelation? There cannot be any simple answer to such a difficult question; however, its complexity itself postulates reflection, and the reflection is to be on man's capacity to change.

Be it as it may about our examples, the issue raised by

our third question is likely to dominate and shape theological reflection for some time to come. Inevitably, it will have an impact on the development of structures and laws as well.

The Evolving Church and the Image of God

The image of God by which the Christian community lives in any given age influences strongly their understanding of mysteries, their perception of the Christian way of life, and their construction of structures and laws.

Such a statement may seem far-fetched. Yet, the more we reflect on various aspects of Christian history, the more we are convinced of it. After all, who could doubt that the Franciscan movement, with all its religious poetry, was inspired mostly by the image of God, tender and compassionate? Or, who would doubt that the movement that brought about the Inquisition originated in a conception of God, terrible in his judgments?

Ultimately, both the articulation of Christian morality and the ways of granting pardon were inspired, at any point of history, by the image that theologians and legislators had of their God. We do not mean, of course, that they simply created a God to their own image. We mean that they received God's self-revelation as mortal human persons, limited in their vision.

We do not comprehend God; we can never reach the depths of his mystery in its simplicity. We learn about him by gathering together small fragments of knowledge that our mind can master, knowledge that points to the ineffable mystery.

At one time, the Christian community rests its gaze on the infinite majesty of the Holy One. Quite naturally, they conclude that God's covenanted people must be holy, too. If someone sins seriously, it is fitting that he should repair the offense given to God, and the wrong done to the community, through public penance. The image of the holy God leads to a harsh and long process of reconciliation.

At another time, the community contemplates the Good Shepherd who is ready to go after the lost sheep not once, not twice, but seventy times seven times. Consequently, they are only too ready to grant mercy whenever an errant sheep is in sight. The image of the God of mercy leads to the easy and frequent granting of pardon.

These reflections could be expanded in many ways, and into many fields. It would certainly be interesting to investigate how far the different models of the Church, or different models of ministry, depended on the image of God that the community possessed at any given time.

Religious persons, Christian or otherwise, are raising the question, implicitly or explicitly, all the time: What kind of person is our God? The answer they find always marks their lives.

Such reflections are demanding. They imply that fitting structures and wise laws must be grounded in a better understanding of our God.

Acknowledgments

The material contained in this book was first offered as a graduate course to students in liturgy and canon law. At the end of the semester, one of them asked, "Can you tell us about all those who influenced your thoughts?" We obviously could not, not without adding another week to the semester! There are only too many to whom we are indebted. Some of them, however, should be singled out. Our memory goes back to those who were our teachers in theology at Collège St. Albert, that was the French-speaking section of the Jesuit college at Louvain. They did more than help us acquire theological knowledge; they launched us on the adventure of exploring God's mighty deeds. Several of them, Pierre Charles, Gustave Lambert, Jean Levie, René Carpentier, Léopold Malevez and others are in God's peace, but their names live on among theologians. They certainly made their contribution to the process of evolution in the Church. At Louvain, too, we became acquainted with the writings of Joseph Maréchal. They woke us gradually, and not without some reluctance on our part, from a kind of dogmatic slumber. The reading of the works of others of the same school (if a school it is) such as Karl Rahner, Emerich Coreth, Joseph de Finance and, in particular, Bernard Lonergan prompted us to move further.

Our bibliography indicates some authors whom we found helpful in one way or another: some helped us with their questions, some with their answers.

But much of what is in the book was not just material for an academic discourse. It was discussed far and wide with Christians serving God and man on different continents, in so many different walks of life. Their insights, too, helped greatly in shaping our thoughts.

To all of these people, we are indebted. To all of them, we offer our thanks.

Let us proceed, now, to our first question.

I

First Question about History: How Did the Practice of Reconciling Sinners Develop?

The goal before our eyes is to build an understanding of the evolving nature of the Church through the development of the sacrament of penance.

This process of understanding must be well grounded in the knowledge of those historical events that marked the development of the rite of pardon in the community. Once we know the changes that have taken place, we are disposed to raise the question of how those changes should be explained.

From the beginning, a possible misconception must be eliminated. Change by way of evolution is never the material addition of one element upon another, as one brick is put on another when a house is built. Nowhere throughout this study do we propose such an idea. Rather, we are concerned with organic growth. The right analogy, if there must be one, is that of the seed which grows into a tree. The tree is potentially present in the seed, yet it is unrecognizable to the observing eye. Between the beginning and the end, the seed and the tree, there is the mysterious process of life that preserves the identity of the plant and yet changes it from season to season. We do not know of any metaphor that illustrates better the harmony of permanent identity and ongoing development in living beings.

The small seed, from which a veritable mustard tree sprouted, was the awareness of the early Christian community that full power over the kingdom was given to the apostles. To Peter first:

> I will give you the keys of the kingdom of heaven, and whatever you bind on earth shall be bound in heaven, and whatever you loose on earth shall be loosed in heaven (Mt 16:19).

And then to the disciples:

> Truly, I say to you, whatever you bind on earth shall be bound in heaven, and whatever you loose on earth shall be loosed heaven (Mt 18:18).

The power "to bind and to loose" is a typical example of the literary form that expresses totality by two extremes; that is, full power was granted, including the right to forgive sins.

John's first letter expresses this awareness:

> If we say we have no sin in us, we are deceiving ourselves and refusing to admit the truth; but if we acknowledge our sins, then God who is faithful and just will forgive our sins and purify us from everything that is wrong (1 Jn 1:8-9).

John's gospel goes further; it says that forgiveness is granted through the ministry of the apostles who are sent by the risen Christ, as Christ was sent by his Father, to forgive sins. Jesus breathed on the apostles and said:

> Receive the Holy Spirit. For those whose sins you forgive, they are forgiven; for those whose sins you retain, they are retained (Jn 20:22-23).

The apostolic Church had a substantial understanding of the way of life taught by Christ. Its members knew what was right and what was wrong, although they certainly did not come to a systematic elaboration of moral theology. Much of their teaching about morality consisted in referring to the example of Christ, and to his sayings, as they were witnessed by the first disciples. Also, they were aware that, if anyone sinned, he could be forgiven through the ministry of the Church. But, we find no evidence in the New Testament of any well-determined rite for pardon. Consequently, the Church had to develop "sacred signs" for the reconciliation of sinners.

Much of the history of the sacrament of penance is an account of the evolution of such a rite. Surprisingly enough, there were two distinct points of departure: one, right from the beginning, in the churches around the Mediterranean; the other, from the fifth century, in the churches in Ireland.

The Mediterranean system was built on a strong consciousness of the unity of the community. Penance was public. It was done in the midst of the community. Reconciliation, granted by the bishop, was part of public liturgy.

The Irish system was built mainly on an understanding that sin was a break in the relationship with God. The priest had to be a discreet, and often secret, minister of reconciliation between God and his erring creature. The rite was structured accordingly.

Such different approaches were bound to come into conflict, and they did. The more practical than theoretical search for a uniform discipline lasted for centuries and came to a solid conclusion at Lateran Council IV in 1225. But the final seal of approval of a system of strongly Irish inspiration was granted by the Council of Trent in 1551.

Our intention is not to recount this history that has been well told by others.[1] But, we want to recall the high points of development so that we become aware of the extent of the changes that have taken place, and of the significance

---

[1] See, e.g., the writings of Amann, Anciaux, Galtier, Palmer, Poschmann, Rahner and Vogel in our bibliography.

of building up in ourselves an understanding of the dynamics of development. The greater the changes have been in the past, the more freedom we are likely to have in the future. We have experienced many times the liberating effect of the study of history. Often, what is believed to be the rigidity of a traditional standpoint is nothing else than the narrow perception of recent centuries.

(1) THE MEDITERRANEAN PATTERN OF THE PROCESS OF FORGIVENESS

In the first five centuries, the particular churches around the Mediterranean developed structures through which forgiveness was granted by the bishop in the midst of the community. Such structures were modeled after the ancient procedure, used by the Jews, of excluding a sinner from the synagogue and admitting him again when he repented. Although Christian practices differed from one place to another, by the fourth or fifth century a fairly uniform pattern had developed. It was followed, also, by the new churches on the continent of Europe.

An important clue **to** the understanding of this Mediterranean rite of granting forgiveness is found in the rule that, to be a penitent, the sinner had to be admitted into the "order of penitents." When this happened, he was marked for life: once a penitent, always a penitent. He became subject to a special and severe discipline.

He could be received into this penitential way of life by the bishop, and by him alone. From the moment he was accepted, he contracted ecclesial and civil disabilities. He was barred for life from clerical service. In many churches, he was forbidden to marry or, if he was married, he was enjoined not to use his marital rights. In the civil society, access to public and honorable offices was closed to him.

After admission into the order of penitents, the repentant sinner had to complete the satisfaction imposed on him by the bishop. This could be manifold. It may have included prayer, fasting, almsgiving and other good deeds. He was assigned a lowly place among the faithful, especially during the Eucharistic service. As he progressed in "paying his debts," that is, in doing his penance, he advanced toward reconciliation. His progress was symbolized by moving closer to the altar in the worshiping community until eventually, his satisfaction completed, the bishop received him into full communion. But, all did not end there. In many ways he continued to be a penitent, and several disabilities remained. If he failed again, no reconciliation was given to him, as a rule, until the time of his imminent death.

Here a question naturally arises: for what kind of sins was someone condemned to do such drastic penance? There was no uniform answer. In many churches, especially in the larger ones, lists evolved containing sins for which the bishop could admit someone into the order of penitents. The lists were of different lengths. All of them contained major offenses, such as apostasy from faith, murder and adultery, but none of them stopped there.[2]

---

[2]The statement "there were only three mortal sins in the early Church, apostasy, murder and adultery" is incorrect on more than one count. It assumes that a precise differentiation between "venial" and "mortal" sins had already taken place in the early Church. This was not the case, although there was an awareness that sins were of different gravity, some of them being capable of bringing eternal death to those who committed them. But such gravity was by no means restricted to those three, as the apostolic literature abundantly testifies.

Often, the sins listed were of a general character, such as doing harm to one's neighbor, being greedy or jealous, and so forth. In practice, it was left to the bishop to judge how much injury or what degree of jealousy or greed warranted public penance. It was more an existential than a scientific approach. The bishop had both to judge the gravity of the sin and to impose the satisfaction accordingly.

It is understandable that such a demanding process was not thought suitable for young persons. Particular councils enjoined bishops not to accept them as penitents. The consequences would have been too harsh for them. Often enough, clerics were barred from doing public penance. Nor were civil officials much seen among penitents. As a rule, the penitents were not numerous, just a small fraction of the community.

But, what about the vast majority of Christian people? Were they unaware of their sins? Quite the contrary. They had a strong awareness of their sinfulness. Anyone who doubts should read early Christian prayers. The very liturgies of the Eucharist are replete with confession of sinfulness and petition for mercy. But, they sought forgiveness through other means than the doing of public penance. They prayed for pardon, they gave alms, they fasted—above all, they implored God's mercy through the Eucharist.

There is simply no historical evidence that Christians went to confession in the way we understand that practice today. Even when someone asked the bishop to be received into the order of penitents, he was not required to make a formal and precise accounting of his sinful deeds. The bishop used his own discretion to decide if the person deserved to be penitent. He could do so on his own general knowledge, or on the reputation of the person in the city, or after inquiring into his way of life—from him or from others.

At the beginning of his satisfaction, the penitent had to confess his sinfulness, in general terms, to the community. Such confession, however, was not meant to be the revelation of his hidden sins.

Cases in which a Christian was compelled, by bishops or canonical penalties, to do public penance were rare. Forced entry into the order of penitents was rather frowned on than encouraged. Personal conversion was considered always the starting point for repentance.

The Mediterranean pattern displayed the unshaken conviction that sinners can be forgiven in community, and the bishop was the legitimate instrument of God's pardon. But, the ways of administering the process exhibited such extreme severity that the vast majority of Christians turned away from it. Eventually, by the end of the fifth and throughout the sixth century, the practice of public penance was dwindling away. The communities remained without a universally recognized and easily available form of obtaining the signs of God's forgiveness.

Some authors claim that, side by side with the all too visible practice of public penance, there must have been secret reconciliations granted by the bishop to persons who were not able to "enter" the order of penitents, and that those reconciliations must have been close to the pattern of our modern confession. Such a thesis, if it refers to ordinary practice and not the care of the dying, is not supported by solid historical evidence.

(2) THE PATTERN OF FORGIVENESS THAT DEVELOPED IN IRELAND

The Irish church, ever since its foundation in the fifth century, was aware of the same facts that prompted so much development around the Mediterranean: Christians do sin, and they can obtain forgiveness through the ministry of the Church. But, due mainly to the strong monastic spirit of the Irish communities, the structure of the process of forgiveness developed in a different way. The Irish created their own signs and symbols.

They had no "order of penitents." Anyone could ask the bishop, or a priest, for God's pardon. The repentant sinner was not segregated from the community, nor was he asked to do penance in public. Once he confessed his sins in private, a satisfaction was imposed on him, often a harsh one, to be done in private.

In earlier times, reconciliation was granted when the penitent returned and reported that he had "satisfied" for his sins. Later, absolution was given right after the confession of sins. No one was marked for having done penance, nor did he incur any ecclesial or civic disability. In fact, all remained hidden, a secret transaction between the priest and the penitent. If someone failed again, he could ask for forgiveness without delay, and he could do so any number of times.

The confession of sins was not understood to be "of the essence" of the penitential rite, but it was considered necessary to assess the right amount of satisfaction.[3] To

---

[3]To speak of the essential elements of the sacrament before the age of the scholastics could be, easily, an anachronism. In fact, the elements of

guide the priest in calculating the penance, abundant literature developed in the so-called "penitential books." In reality, they were dictionaries of all conceivable sins in all imaginable circumstances, indicating the right amount of expiation for each.

The marked contrast between this simple process and the elaborate Mediterranean pattern is immediately apparent. Penance was not restricted to any type of sin, as it was not restricted to any kind of people. Pardon was available for all sins, great and small. Anyone could request it every time he needed it, without regard to his age, sex or social position.

The Irish church created new signs, symbols and structures. They were less rigid than those used on the continent. They were more adaptable to the needs of all kinds of people, men and women, young and old, weak and strong. The satisfactions imposed were harsh, but they could be done in secret; there was no need for publicity.[4] The sacrament was made even more accessible by the fact that absolution was not reserved to the bishop; it could be granted by a priest.

The two systems, the Mediterranean and the Irish, had common foundations: both were built on the belief that pardon for sins can be obtained in the Christian community through the ministry of bishops or priests. But, they displayed strong differences as to whom, by whom, in what way, and how many times pardon could be given.

the rite kept changing; the content that they signified remained the same.

[4] The harshness of penances was mitigated by a custom that gradually developed. They could be shared with others. Members of the household, friends, even persons hired for this specific purpose, could take on some of the penances of the master—who thus had much less to do. A living demonstration of the faith in the unity of the Church!

Sooner or later, the two systems were bound to come into conflict.

They did when Irish priests crossed over to the European continent, as pilgrims and missionaries, carrying in their minds their own understanding of the administration of forgiveness, and in their bags their penitential books. The stage was set for them: most Christians on the continent were already alienated from the use of public penance. The Irish offered pardon to them in a new form with no public and permanent humiliation attached to it.

People responded positively. They must have been longing to know about God's forgiveness and to obtain it through visible and sacred signs. The Irish filled this need. The new practice expanded rapidly.

But there was some loss, too. The awareness of the social dimension of sin and repentance diminished significantly. The emphasis was on the personal reconciliation of a Christian with his Maker.

We should note also that the Irish had a new understanding as to what sins could or should be submitted to the priest: any and all; they conceived of no restrictions. They had no short list of sins in their churches; rather, they had the mass of sins listed in their penitential books. All of them were bad, but all could be forgiven provided there was proper satisfaction done. A truly new situation had arisen: for the first time, all sins, small or great, public or secret, were associated with the penitential procedure.

(3) THE CONFLICT

Difference in understanding leads easily to external conflict. By the end of the sixth century, there was indeed a difference in understanding of the ways a sinner could obtain forgiveness in the Church. The source of one conception was in the Mediterranean churches; from there, it spread to the newly converted peoples in the north. The source of another conception was in the churches of Ireland; from there, it was brought, by pilgrim priests, to the European continent.

External conflict became inevitable. It lasted for some five centuries, with varying intensity. The two systems were too different to coexist peacefully side by side. Two conciliar texts, in clear contrast with each other, can be quoted to illustrate the opposing minds and practices.

One text is from the Third Council of Toledo held in 589. It was a particular, but important, council. Sixty-two bishops participated; the recently converted king of the Visigoths, Rekkared, was present also. There a number of Arian bishops were reconciled, and the unity of the Church was restored. The king and the Fathers made solemn profession of their faith according to the Councils of Nicea, Constantinople I and Chalcedon. To safeguard the purity of faith, the Council issued twenty-three doctrinal statements and another twenty-three disciplinary *capitula*. The eleventh is on penance:[5]

> We have learned that, throughout some churches [*parishes and/or dioceses*] of Spain, the faithful are doing penance not according to the canonical rule but in another detestable way. That is, as many times as it

---

[5] All quotations that follow, throughout this chapter, are our own translations. We tried to remain as faithful to the original text as it was possible to do, without losing its meaning. When it was necessary for the sake of clarity, we added a few explanatory words in brackets; they are printed in italics.

pleases them to sin, they ask a presbyter to grant them pardon.

We want to put an end to such an abominable presumption. [*Therefore,*] this sacred council orders that penances be given according to the rite [*procedure*] prescribed by the ancient canons: that is, that the person who repents of his evil deeds be excluded temporarily from Eucharistic communion and, along with other penitents, ask often for the imposition of hands; and that, when the time of his satisfaction is completed according to the judgment of the bishop, he be readmitted to communion.

Those who relapse into their sins, either while doing penance or after they have been reconciled, must be condemned according to the severity of the ancient canons (*Concilium Toletanum III, capitulum* 11; Mansi, *Conciliorum collectio,* vol. 9, col. 995).

The discussions of the bishops have not been recorded for us, but the terms used by them give some indication of their mood and attitude. They saw nothing of value in the Irish practice; they called it detestable. They must have thought of it as an illegitimate innovation, otherwise their sweeping condemnation makes no sense. Had they been aware of an ancient tradition of private confessions followed by private absolutions, they could not have spoken in such violent terms.

The other text is from a council held at Chalon-sur-Saone, in the province of Lyons. In the middle of the seventh century (between 647 and 653), the bishops of the western kingdoms of the Franks gathered there in synod. They professed their faith according to the Nicean Creed and, as a fruit of their deliberations, they promulgated twenty-seven disciplinary decrees. Canon 8 not only upheld the Irish penitential system but positively recommended it, although in discreet terms:

> We judge that penance for sins is a medicine for the soul; it is good for all. All priests agree that once the penitent has confessed his sins to the priest, he should be given his penance (*Concilium Cabilonense,* canon 8; Mansi: vol. 10, col. 1191).

Again, there is no way of reconstructing the discussions that led to such a decision, but the tone of the text is quiet and simple. It does not betray any kind of apprehension about following the new practice instead of the old. This fact is all the more remarkable since the synod was preoccupied with upholding the authority of the bishops, the right government of monasteries, and, in general, the purity of Christian morals. Yet, it described penance in its new form as the remedy of the soul, and good for all. The priests were simply directed to receive the confessions of the faithful and to impose appropriate penances. The bishops implicitly renounced, in favor of all priests, their exclusive right to reconcile sinners.

Two synods; two minds. One rigidly upholding the old idea and discipline; the other firmly recommending the new understanding and practice. Certainly, they both tried to fulfill the evangelical mandate: go and proclaim God's mercy. But, they differed over the way of doing it.

Gradually, the tide turned in favor of the Irish system. The faithful abandoned the practice of public penance; people flocked to those priests who gave them absolution privately.

Poschmann, the well-known historian of the sacrament of penance, observes:

> By the end of the ancient Christianity, the evolution of canonical penance has come to a dead end. The increasing hardening of its procedure has lent it a utopian purpose: that is, to impose sooner or later on all the faithful a kind of monastic renouncement of the world. The result of such demand was that the faithful in practice discarded ecclesiastical penance from their life, and considered it nearly exclusively as a means to prepare themselves for death (cf. Bernhard Poschmann, *Penance and the Anointing of the Sick,* p. 123).

Further:

> At the same time that the Fathers of the Council [*of Toledo*] pronounced their verdict on private penance, the very same practice began its triumphal march over the European continent (cf. *ibid.,* p. 124).

If one form of discipline has come to a dead end and another begun its march, the judgment of the whole Church, of bishops, priests and faithful must have been that the two rites were, indeed, significantly different.[6]

---

[6]Poschmann curiously contradicts himself. A few pages later, in the same book, he states:

> . . . The introduction of the new penitential procedure is accomplished without conflict or resistance, notwithstanding the strong condemnation that the innovation provoked at the Third Council of Toledo. There is no evidence that the Celtic monks introduced a modification (cf. Poschmann, *Penance,* p. 132).

After he weighs the evidence available from mainly canonical sources, he finds new confirmation:

> In fact, in the new procedure [*discipline*], [*the contemporaries*] did not see anything new. On the contrary, they saw the

The following centuries have seen a long struggle to find a compromise and a new balance.

(4) ATTEMPTS AT RESTORATION: A NEW BALANCE THAT WAS A COMPROMISE

Change did not come easily to the Church of the early Middle Ages; it hardly ever does come easily. True, the new way of obtaining pardon, by private confession to a priest and satisfaction done secretly, filled a need and attracted many. Yet, it went against ancient traditions, and *they* had to be kept intact!

The ninth century was the time of a great reform movement carried on under the watchful eyes, and with the willing cooperation, of Emperor Charlemagne. Discipline had to be restored everywhere, in worship, in monastic life—also, in the way pardon was granted to the sinner.

At Chalon-sur-Saone, the bishops of southern France gathered again in 813. They were in a different mood from their predecessors who had encouraged the new penitential practice a century and a half earlier. Now, the old practice

continuation and the perfecting of the old discipline (cf. *ibid.,* p. 134).

In upholding this thesis of "no significant change," Poschmann is representative of a whole group of historians of dogma such as Amann, Anciaux, Galtier, Palmer and others.

In our opinion, while their works are admirable in presenting the events through which developments have taken place, they have no adequate understanding of the dynamics of change, especially of the development of doctrine and of the evolution of the capacity of human persons to know. Since their grasp of these dynamic factors is insufficient, they have no other way of preserving continuity of belief than by claiming a greater identity between historical situations than is actually warranted by historical facts. They are excellent in observing external changes, but their perception of underlying trends, which produce the changes, is insufficient.

had to be restored.

Accordingly, they determined:

> In most places the practice of doing penance according to the ancient canons has died out; nor is the old rule about reconciliation observed.

> The help of the Lord Emperor should be sought [*to restore the previous order, so that*] if anyone has sinned publicly he should be punished by public penance and according to the canons, as he deserves it, he should be excommunicated and reconciled (*Concilium Cabilonense II,* canon 25; Mansi: vol. 14, col. 98).

The root of the trouble was, obviously, in the penitential books that were rapidly multiplying everywhere. So, those books were the object of another decree:

> Penance must be imposed on those who confess their sins either according to the norms of ancient canons, or according to the authority of the sacred scriptures, or according to ecclesiastical customs . . .

> The so-called penitential books, filled with evident errors and composed by unworthy authors, must be repudiated and totally eliminated . . . (*Concilium Cabilonense II,* canon 38; Mansi: vol. 14, col. 101).

A regional Council of Paris, in 829, goes further. It directs the bishops to search for the penitential books and to have them all burned:

> Many priests, partly by negligence, partly by ignorance, do not follow canon law when they impose penances on those who confess their guilt. [*Such*

priests] use for their guides certain books composed against canonical authorities; they are the so-called penitential books. By their action, they do not heal the wounds of sin, they rather make their condition worse . . . Rightfully, we all agree [*and decree*] that every bishop should order a diligent search for those books full of errors. When they are found, he should have them burned so that no more ignorant priests can deceive the faithful (*Concilium Parisiense, caput* 32; Mansi: vol. 14, col. 559).

The real conflict, however, was not between the ancient canons and the new penitential books. It was between the minds; on the one side, minds rooted in tradition but not able to distinguish between the core of Christian belief and its culturally and historically conditioned expression; on the other side, a perception of the genuine tradition that remains the same and evolves in new forms.[7]

As a matter of fact, the attempt at restoration was not successful, not even "with the help of the emperor." The Irish practice could not be uprooted anymore. The penitential books continued to multiply, and the new discipline was spreading further.

Out of the conflict, a new balance emerged in the form of an enduring yet precarious compromise. A new rule emerged: public penance should be done for public and notorious wrongdoing; private penance was allowed for secret sins. A monk and theologian of mid-ninth century, Hrabanus Maurus, the so-called first teacher of Germany,

[7]If anyone complains today about confusion concerning the sacrament of penance, he should be told about the times when one diocese was continuing the struggle to restore the discipline of public expiation, while another was administering forgiveness through a discreet encounter with the priest. That conflict was not cleared up in a short time either.

in his book *On the Formation of Clerics,* sums up concisely the new doctrine:

> Those who have sinned publicly must do penance publicly, for as many seasons as the bishop determines it, according to the gravity of the sins of each penitent. [*Such penitents*] must be reconciled publicly by the bishop or by the presbyters [*although by the order of the bishop*] as the African councils decreed where it is written:
>
>> Any penitent who was guilty of public and known crime that was a scandal for the whole Church should be reconciled by the imposition of hands before the sanctuary . . .
>
> Those who have sinned secretly and revealed their sins in spontaneous confession to the presbyter or to the bishop only, must be given a secret penance according to the judgment of the presbyter or the bishop to whom they confessed, so that the weak members of the Church should not be scandalized [*as they would be*] if they saw someone doing penance without knowing why (Rabanus Maurus. *De clericorum institutione, Liber II, caput* 30; Migne, *Patrologia Latina,* vol. 107, cols. 342-343).

But, the practice of public penance had been weakening ever since the fifth century, and the cause of private penance had been advancing. Not even the neat rule of doing public penance for public sins, and private penance for private sins, could alter the general direction of the development.

It was not always easy to decide what was public. A fault could be well-known in one place, not so in another. Besides, the system was unpopular. Eventually the twofold discipline evolved into a threefold system. Robert of Flamborough describes it in his *Penitential Book,* a *summa* for confessors, published around 1210. He writes:

> There are three kinds of penance: public penance with liturgical solemnity; public penance with no solemnity; and private penance.

> Public penance with liturgical solemnity is the one given at the beginning of Lent when the sinner takes ceremonially the penitential robe and the ashes, and is ejected from the community. It is called public because he does it publicly . . . The public penance without liturgical solemnity is done openly [*in facie ecclesiae*] such as penitential pilgrimage. Private penance is done any day, privately, before the priest.

> Solemn public penance can be imposed only by the bishop or someone authorized by him . .. Public penance and private penance is granted by a priest at any time (*Liber poenitentialis,* ed. Francis Firth. Toronto: Pontifical Institute of Medieval Studies, 1971. p. 205).

(5) THE CANONIZATION OF THE PRESENTLY VALID RITE BY THE COUNCILS OF LATERAN IV AND TRENT

We are not speaking anymore of new historical developments, not as far as the sacramental sign is concerned. We are speaking of the granting of full and exclusive canonical validity to the rite of private confession and absolution, for the whole Western Church, by the Councils of Lateran IV in 1215 and Trent (Session 14) in 1551.

The Lateran Council "determined" that:

Each faithful, of either sex, once having reached the age of discretion, must confess, sincerely, alone, once a year at least, all his sins, to his own priest. He should then fulfill, as his strength allows, the penance that has been imposed, and receive reverently, at Easter at least, the sacrament of the Eucharist . . . (*Concilium Lateranense IV, cap.* 21; Denzinger-Schoenmetzer, ed. 34, 812).

This canon is usually referred to as the one introducing a duty of annual confession and communion. That is correct. But, there is more behind the text than what meets the eye in reading it.

By imposing the annual duty of confession, the highest teaching and legislative body of the Church acknowledged the full validity of the rite that originated in Ireland, and tacitly ratified the disappearance of the Mediterranean system. The climate had changed a great deal since earlier centuries. There was no attempt, on the part of the bishops, to restore the old canonical discipline; they imposed yearly confession on all. Such a universal obligation of annual penance would have been inconceivable and unacceptable within the system of the "order of penitents." In an oblique way, the Council froze the structure of the sacramental sign as it existed in 1215.

The Council of Trent did not change the rite of pardon any further. It ratified, again, what had been done by the Fathers of Lateran IV. Many of the discussions at Trent were in function of the reformers' denial of the sacramental nature of penance and, consequently, of its internal capacity to confer the grace of pardon and healing through the ministry of the Church. The complex discussions do not concern us here.

The rite of Irish origin was solemnly approved by the Fathers:

> . . . the universal Church always held that the Lord instituted the full confession of sins . . . and that it exists as necessary, by divine law, for all those who have lapsed after their baptism (cf. canon 7).

> Our Lord Jesus Christ, before he ascended from this world into heaven, designated priests as his own vicars, that they should be presidents and judges to whom all mortal sins [*crimina*], into which the faithful may have fallen, should be submitted. They should judge, in virtue of the power of the keys, if sins should be remitted or retained. Clearly, the priests cannot pronounce such judgment without being properly informed about the cause, nor could they observe equity in imposing penalties if the faithful made a general confession only and did not disclose their sins by their precise names, one by one (Denzinger-Schoenmetzer, ed. 34, 1679).

After the Council of Trent, there was virtually no evolution in the structure of the rite of pardon, that is, in the sacramental sign.

(6) A CONCLUSION

Having observed the historical process, we ask; what conclusion can we draw from it? What is the theological significance of the changes?

Three different interpretations or hypotheses can be proposed.

(a) The first hypothesis: an inauthentic evolution has been superseded by an authentic one. The Mediterranean system was the inauthentic one; the one introduced by the Irish, the authentic one.

Such an interpretation of history cannot be accepted. It would be absurd to assume that the communities of the Mediterranean churches developed a practice that was a deviation from the heritage they received from the Lord. What they did may not have been the perfect expression of the use of the power of pardon, but it could not have been sheer aberration, either.

(b) The second hypothesis: the earlier system was an imperfect development that was perfected by the later one.

This interpretation is attractive since it assumes organic evolution. But, it assumes, also, that there can be only one correct expression of the tradition. If one practice is supplanted by another, the later one must be the perfecting of the earlier one.

The fact stands that the Fathers of several particular councils perceived a significant difference between the two systems; they did not think that one was perfecting the other. Every condemnation of the "new" was an implicit—but resounding—approval of the "old." It would be idle to pretend that, during the period of conflict, the bishops saw an organic unity unfolding.

(c) The third hypothesis: both systems were authentic expressions of the apostolic tradition. Each was conceived in function of the spiritual needs of the community, in different cultural contexts. In each, there was an authentic interpretation of the use of the power granted by the Lord to his disciples. Yet, neither was perfect; each displayed certain limitations.

We accept the third hypothesis as the correct theological interpretation of the historical changes. The reason is that, at one time or another, each system had the support of the universal Church, certainly of the universal episcopate. The opposing views were not about the permanent core of the sacrament, but about its temporary historical expression—even if the bishops did not quite realize it. The conflict, therefore, must not be explained as the fight of the authentic *versus* the inauthentic, nor as the fight of the perfect against the imperfect, but as a struggle between two genuine, but limited, expressions of Christian tradition.[8]

Such a conclusion will affect the rest of this study. If there were two authentic expressions of one tradition, it is

---

[8]We are well aware of the opinion of those writers who hold that the most significant changes in the development of the rite of penance did not take place in the transition from the Mediterranean to the Irish system, but in the transition from the regime of the Penitentials to the practice of modern auricular confessions. Most recently Thomas Tentler writes in his *Sin and Confession on the Eve of the Reformation:*

> Despite the open clash between these systems [*canonical penance and the Penitentials*], however, they were fundamentally similar. The great contrast exists not between canonical penance and the penitentials, but between both of them and the system of private penance that was to rule the church from the twelfth and thirteenth centuries to the present (p. 10).

We accept that there is a contrast between the present system of private penance and the system of Penitentials (who could doubt that?), but in our judgment, there is an even greater overall contrast between the system of canonical penance and that of the Penitentials. The degree of difference, after all, will remain a matter of judgment and cannot be precisely measured.

We would like to stress, however, a judgment that radical changes have taken place in the evolution of penance in the twelfth and thirteenth centuries only would not affect the scope of our study. Whether the radical changes are recognized in an earlier or later period, the undeniable fact stands that they have taken place. All that we need to give a solid foundation to the chapters that follow is the knowledge that significant changes have taken place in the course of the development of penance.

legitimate to think of new manifestations of the power of pardon that is present in the Church, unchanged in its substance. Such new manifestations need not be fully identical either with the Mediterranean process or with the rite that originated in Ireland. They could use some elements of both.

A liberating conclusion! We are free to form responsible judgments about the possible courses that future developments should take.

Obviously, we speak of freedom to investigate and to propose, not of license to destroy. We do not deny the binding character of the present structures and laws. As they are, they, too, represent an authentic stage in development. But, we cannot stop; truth and mercy must continue to unfold.

2

Second Question about Ideas: How Do They Change?

In surveying the development of the sacrament of penance, we have found a balance between permanency and change. There has been permanency in the awareness of the Christian community that sins can be forgiven through the ministry of the Church. There have been changes in the signs through which forgiveness has been granted.

Presently, we are interested in the changes. They have been external, visible and tangible. But external changes could not have taken place without internal inspirations that were invisible and intangible. Therefore, if we look for reasons behind the changes, we must find them in the ideas that inspired them.

We use the term "idea" in a general sense: "any product of mental apprehension or activity, existing in the mind as an object of knowledge or thought; an item of knowledge or belief; a thought, conception, notion; a way of thinking" (*The Oxford English Dictionary*). Obviously, we mean a new insight that can be articulated through a concept or a sentence, and can develop into a tentative hypothesis and a critical judgment. Judgments, in their turn, can accumulate into a body of knowledge or, as we often call it, a body of doctrine. By development of ideas, we also mean what is traditionally called the development of doctrine. In sum, we use the term "idea" as a collective noun for the content of diverse mental operations.

The natural link between ideas and external events is so close that we cannot understand external changes unless we understand something of the evolution of ideas or the development of doctrine. Hence, our question: how do ideas develop?

As we watch a human person grow over a period of years we find that, in spite of all changes, at the core of his being he remains the same. He has a permanent identity; he has it from birth to death. Yet, he really grows; he develops physically, mentally, emotionally and spiritually. Under many aspects he does not remain the same. However, his identity is stronger than all of the changes; they cannot destroy it. The permanent core of his person holds together all the developments that take place over the years.

The Church is a living body because it is a community of living persons; hence, it, too, is subject to changes. Yet, at the core of the community there is an identity that is permanent, in spite of all changes. The small and fearful group of disciples of Jesus comforted by the Spirit is identical with the worldwide "gathering" of Christians of today, in spite of all the changes that have taken place over the centuries.

Indeed, the Church has lived through many changes that have gone deeper than the numerical increase in membership or the expansion of the community to the ends of the earth. The understanding of the Christian message developed; from new visions, new practices were born.

The history of the sacrament of penance shows the evolving nature of the Church—with a core of permanent identity. There has always been a quiet and firm conviction that Jesus gave the mysterious power to forgive sins to his apostles and that, consequently, the Church, through its ministers, could grant God's mercy to repentant sinners.

Yet, right from the beginning, the apostolic Church had to find ways and means to signify that sins were forgiven. Eventually a complex pattern of rites and symbols was created around the Mediterranean. Another pattern followed, in the churches of Ireland. But both types of procedures were born from the one conviction: the Church has received a mandate from the Lord to grant pardon to sinners.

The changes in discipline have not done away with the core identity of the group; rather, the opposite is true. It has been the enduring community which has initiated the changes. Its faith was so rich that not any one manifestation could reveal its internal wealth.

Evolution, after all, is a manifestation of life, even in a community of believers. At first sight, there seems to be a contrast, if not a contradiction, between the demands of permanency and change. But such an impression is a superficial one. At the deepest level, every movement of life is the fruit of a balanced play between the forces of stability and the need for mobility. The contrast is already present in the gospels.

Jesus said:

> For truly I say to you, till heaven and earth pass away not an iota, not a dot, will pass from the law until all is accomplished (Mt 5:18).

He also said:

> When the Spirit of truth comes he will guide you into all the truth; . . . (Jn 16:13).

The first saying of Jesus refers to the permanency of God's gifts, to the demands of fidelity. The second speaks of progress in our understanding of the same gifts, of the need to move toward the whole truth.

Fidelity and progress go together. If someone is faithful to the letter of the law, but does not advance in the understanding of its spirit, he fails to recognize a living gift. He treats God's revelation as a lifeless monument to be guarded, revered and preserved intact. If someone is intent on change only, and not attached to the core of the truth, he is like a ship without anchor, tossed about by the waves, turned around by every wind.

Here is our complex duty: we must be faithful to the truth that endures, and follow an understanding that evolves.[1]

But to stand by the truth faithfully, and to move with the new understanding steadily, we need to know something about the relationship between reality, any reality, outside of us, and our capacity to perceive it.[2]

---

[1] The gospels are the memories of the first disciples of Jesus, of his words and deeds. The two sayings quoted above show that the disciples perceived a core, which would endure beyond all changes, in the revelation they received. That core would be like the seed sown in the soil—it would change into a mighty tree. Therefore, they could say that "not a dot" of the Law would pass away. The very same Law would expand and develop, under the guidance of the Spirit, into a fulness that was not there in the beginning.

[2] Here we begin to broach the immense issue of cognitional theory. In order to know what our knowledge represents we must also know how it comes into existence. To guide the reader who is, perhaps, more interested in technical explanation than in parables, let us state our position in philosophical terms.

We cannot accept the naive realism, based strongly on the theory of universal concepts, which assumes that we are able to perceive with our minds the same essence that is in the objects of our knowledge. We cannot accept it, even with the qualification that the *mode* of our representation of the essence is different from the mode of its existence in the object.

We cannot accept the Kantian critique of the mind, either. It grants us certainty only about ideas, mental categories, and space and time as internal forms of our sense perception, but leaves us ignorant concerning the universe that surrounds us.

With those two extremes rejected, where do we stand?

We hold that all authentic knowledge begins with sense perception, but such perception is not a vehicle for the transmission of the *essence* of things. Rather, on the basis of the information received, the mind is

The Parable of Those Who Went to Explore a Mountain

The central issue in our attempt to understand developments in our beliefs and practices is our capacity to know the world around us.

We must beware of two extremes. One is in pretending that our knowledge is merely relative, and not grounded in facts. This is equivalent to denying that God has spoken to us, or that we are able to hear his word and understand it.

The other is in saying that our knowledge is perfect, that we can fathom God's mighty deeds in their fulness. This is to affirm, naively, that we can penetrate into the divine mysteries all at once.

The right approach is somewhere between the two extremes.

To find it, let us begin by telling the parable of the pioneers who went to explore a mountain.[3]

able to generate an understanding that brings meaning into the otherwise disparate data. Thus, there is no true knowledge that does not begin with sense perception. Thus, man has a capacity to generate understanding. Such an approach explains why, on the basis of the same data, different understandings can arise according to the different capacities of persons involved in the process of knowing. Knowledge, then, is the balanced fruit between perceiving what is given to us and finding, through some kind of creative activity, a meaning in it. Such meaning is always subject to further development and correction, and yet it can, at any point, reach a judgment that remains true ever after.

The extremes of naive realism are avoided. While we remain rooted in the real through our sense perception, we do not claim to possess the very essence of things. Therefore, our knowledge remains perfectible.

The extremes of the Kantian stand are avoided. While we admit that there is a contribution of our mind in building up an understanding, we do not consider it detached from the outside world, but rather as originating in it.

Short as this explanation is, for those so interested, it gives an account of our position.

Let us turn to our first parable now.

[3]We ask the learned reader not to hold that our parables are out of place. They are simple, but they may throw light on such a complex

Once upon a time there was a great mountain, and a group of brave men decided to explore it.

The mountain, of course, had been there ever since man could remember, even before he had come to exist. Barring some cosmic catastrophe it would stand there, perhaps, beyond the time allotted to man. Its existence, its nature, its permanence were all objective facts; they did not depend on man's knowledge. But, the explorers could discover the mountain only gradually.

When they first approached it, they looked at the mountain from afar. One day it was shrouded in haze; another, it stood majestically, clear against the sky. But, from a distance, they could give only a general description of its shape, its height and its width, not much more; their report had to be vague. Yet, this report was not merely subjective or purely relative. It just reflected the state of knowledge they were able to gain from the position they had reached.

Then, one day, the men set out to conquer the heights. They formed a team: they wanted a true, scientific exploration. Among them, there were a geographer, a geologist, a botanist and a zoologist. They invited a meteorologist as well; and, to round off the group, they asked a poet and a man of God to join them.

Their climb to the peak was long and arduous. Day by day, they sent back reports to their home base. In fact, each member of the team composed his own, so those at home received varied descriptions of the mountain. One

issue as the emergence of intelligent judgment. After all, did not Einstein explain the lofty theory of relativity, which changed the course of empirical sciences, with such homely experiences as traveling on a train, getting off it and watching it get struck by lightning; or, as going up and down in an elevator? His method should be good enough for us to follow . . . !

explorer spoke of brooks and lakes; another, of geological formations; a third, of plants and trees. A fourth described the animals that appeared on the scene. The meteorologist reported changing patterns of winds and clouds. The poet sent back his rhymes and stanzas about the beauty of nature. The man of God wrote lofty meditations about the manifestation of God's power in creation.

As they climbed, each of the team built up his own understanding of the mountain. None of them was in possession of the full truth, yet each knew fragments of it. None of them described the mountain perfectly, not even according to his own specialty, yet each gave a true account of it according to his capacity.

A fuller image of the mountain could emerge only when all the reports were put together at the end of the exploration. Even then, however, the knowledge of the mountain was not exhaustive. There remained plenty for others to discover, if they wanted to go and explore the mountain further.

Indeed, no matter how much a man learns, his knowledge is never completed. Mostly, it needs to be revised and corrected. Even when he is in possession of all the data, his mind can progress in a better understanding of them.

* * * *

Someone may find the reading of this parable disturbing and ask: is there any room, in this process, for truth? Or, is the search for truth an ongoing, never-ending process? A senseless journey without a goal?

The answer is that a fragment of truth is reached at every moment, but never the full truth. The process is an exploration of the real world, not a flight of fancy. But, there is progress in the process: it is in grasping the facts more firmly so that we can achieve a better understanding of them. Such movement is rooted in facts; there is objectivity in it. It is a process for persons humble enough to acknowledge the limited capacity of their minds which cannot penetrate the whole truth all at once.

The mountain was there before man came to see it. He may explore it over and over again. Yet, presumably, to the end of time it will keep some of its secrets. The understanding of all the forces of nature that operate in it will never be completed by a mortal human being.

The Meaning of the Parable

We are not really concerned with a mountain composed of perishable elements. We are concerned with God's mighty deeds in time and space, in our human history. He has spoken to our fathers in many and various ways. In these last days, he has spoken to us by his son, whom he appointed the heir of all things, through whom also he created the world (cf. Heb 1:1-2).

We are concerned with God's transcendental power and its manifestation in time and space: the power to forgive sins and the process of granting this forgiveness. This power is not mere legal faculty, nor does it originate in any human capacity. It is the strength of God that, once again, heals the sick and brings life to the dead. Through a poor human community, that is the Church, God is manifesting his glory again, not once, or twice, or three times, but every time the Church prays over a repentant sinner.

God's mighty deeds are not perishable, they are part of our own history. They cannot be canceled out. But our understanding of them is limited. We progress in the understanding of his actions, step by step. Each generation of Christians explores God's revelation over and over again. With the help of the Spirit, they understand more and more, they move gradually toward the fulness of truth. God's mighty deeds do not change in time, nor do his mysteries. Our comprehension of them evolves. We are progressing toward the fulness of truth, a fulness that is not given to us to reach in this life.[4]

This is precisely what has happened in the course of history, regarding the sacrament of penance. God's own love for the repentant sinner has not changed as the centuries have gone by. It is as fresh today as it was when Jesus first revealed it to "a woman of the city who was a sinner" but "loved much" (cf. Lk 7:36-50), or to the "chief tax collector" who "sought to see who Jesus was . . . and climbed up into a sycamore tree to see him" (cf. Lk 19:1-10). Its extent could not be fully grasped by the first generation of Christians; there was room for more discovery as the Church evolved.

There is no reason to think that we have come to a point where we must stop. Indeed, by all calculations based on

---

[4]In the words of Vatican Council II:

This tradition which comes from the apostles develops in the Church with the help of the Holy Spirit. For there is a growth in the understanding of the realities and the words which have been handed down. This happens through the contemplation and study made by believers, who treasure these things in their hearts (cf. Lk 2:19, 51), through the intimate understanding of spiritual things they experience, and through the preaching of those who have received through episcopal succession the sure gift of truth. For, as the centuries succeed one another, the Church constantly moves forward toward the fullness of divine truth until the words of God reach their complete fulfillment in her (*Constitution on Divine Revelation, Dei Verbum,* #8).

faith and reason, the discoveries will continue to the end of time. To know that God's kingdom is much richer than what we can grasp of it here and now should be a cause for rejoicing.

A deficiency in our parable, however, should be stressed. The exploration of the mountain can be done through human effort. The knowledge of it can be built up with the help of earthly resources. Not so with the understanding of God's mighty deeds in our history. There he must prompt us to move, he must sustain us throughout the journey, and he alone can lead us to the right conclusion.

It follows, therefore, that the evolution of ideas or the doctrinal development that has taken place in the Christian community should not be looked at simply as the fruit of human ingenuity or the product of different cultural forces. Granted that all those have been at work, ultimately the Spirit of God is behind the changes. Therefore, no change is alien to us. Each carries a meaning, even if it is difficult for us to decipher it. Even heretics played their part in building new understandings of the old message. The questions they raised were often good and pertinent. They went wrong in their answers, and broke away from the common faith. But, it would have been difficult to raise good questions without the Spirit!

No one should ever be afraid to examine changes. In the history of Christian thought the periods of quiet growth, no less than the surprising developments, reveal something of the ways and person of the Spirit.

This is true, of course, in the case of the sacrament of penance. Through learning about its history, we learn about the ways of the Spirit. Gradually, as we understand him better, we learn to work with him more closely.[5]

New Insights Are the Source of All External Changes

There would have been no change in the external pattern of granting forgiveness to the sinner had not Christians, bishops, priests, laypersons conceived new insights about the process. New ideas were at the source of the external changes.

Ideas are living beings because they are generated by living persons. They are not like clothes put on, but proceed from the innermost part of our being. Once conceived, they have a life of their own. They take shape and,

[5]The statement brings us back to the idea that dominates this study from beginning to end, although it is expressed only occasionally. All our theological insights, all our practical norms are rooted in our image of God, that is in our understanding of God's own personality, of his thoughts and ways.

Books have been written about the models that influenced, in various ways throughout the course of history, our understanding of the Church and the ways the life of the Christian community was organized. The study could be carried further and the question raised as to why a given model was followed by the community. The answer would be, of course, because either the community as a whole, or those in charge of it, perceived God as someone particularly pleased with the model. Therefore, the real history of development is not so much in the succession or reconciliation of various models, useful as they can be for our understanding, but in the evolving understanding of who our God is, what it is that pleases him, what it is that is an acceptable offering to him.

Such study would require the cooperation of theologians, historians, and of specialists in the practical life of the Church as expressed in liturgical norms or structural and disciplinary laws. As long as each one follows his own specialty circumscribed narrowly and precisely, it is difficult to explore a common source of questions.

Team work is common now in all fields of empirical sciences. Without it not much can be achieved. In the field of theology there is no less a need for a cooperative effort, but we are still far away from its realization.

sooner or later, come to light. Then they grow, reach full development and, finally, either achieve immortality of a sort, or decline and die. They are hardly ever mere abstractions floating around, strangers to the real world with no relation to the flow of tangible things. Apart from sheer flights of fancy, ideas are rooted in the world and shape the world. They represent the real existing world and, in a mysterious way, they have the capacity to transform reality into their own image.

Ideas shape the life of the Church, too; they make their impact on the life of believers.

The churches around the Mediterranean had their own conception of the process of obtaining forgiveness in community, and they established the practice of public penance accordingly. The churches in Ireland, starting fresh, had new insights into the working of God's mercy in individuals, and thus they initiated the practice of private confessions.

To understand the changing Church, we must raise more questions about the movement of ideas:

(1) How are ideas born?
(2) How do they live?
(3) What is authentic and inauthentic development?

(1) HOW IDEAS ARE BORN; OR, THE OUTLINE OF A COGNITIONAL THEORY

All The Information About the Mountain Comes From Outside

The source for the conception or generation of ideas is in factual information from the outside about any given subject or situation. The information can be adequate or fragmentary; it can be self-explanatory or desperately puzzling. It may point to an obvious meaning, or suggest latent causes for some happening. Be that as it may, such information in itself is not enough. Our mind cries out for the understanding of facts and events. We want more than to receive data passively; we want to know actively.

Thus, we cannot be satisfied with simply storing the information about the practices of the Mediterranean churches, of the churches of Ireland, and of the universal Church in later ages. Our mind is more than a filing cabinet for facts and events. We want to understand, to know, why such significant changes have taken place.

All The Understanding About The Mountain Springs From Inside

Following its desire to know, our mind moves into the scenes presented to it. It penetrates beyond the surface of things, beyond the simple succession of events. It absorbs the available information, screens it, shifts it, reorders it, according to the importance of the elements contained in it.

Soon we are able to raise questions about existing cohesions, underlying causes, laws governing events, and so forth. In short, we are on our way toward understanding. Eventually, on the basis of the data available, our mind generates an insight that brings order into disorder, purposefulness into seemingly erratic movements.[6] Then

⁶"To generate" an insight is a more correct expression than "to create" an insight. Our preference goes to the first, although sometimes, even for the sake of style, we use the second. In truth, both expressions are

we understand.

Thus, as we survey the facts of penitential practices in the Mediterranean churches in the first centuries, we come to understand that, at the source of the process, there was a deep realization of the social dimension of both sin and forgiveness; it was the task of the whole community to restore the sinner to his innocent state again. As we review the Irish penitential rites, we come to see that, at their origin, there was a belief that sin is primarily, or overwhelmingly, a break of relationship with the immensely holy God; for them, the role of the priest was to heal the breach between the Holy One and sinful man. From then on, the differences between the two systems make better sense to us.

Yet, even if we are able to reach some understanding, our mind cannot penetrate all the data with one stroke, right to their greatest depths. The search for the right meaning hidden in fragmentary information is, more often than not, like fishing. The net must be thrown many times before it comes up with a good catch. The reflective mind creates different hypotheses and tests them, one after the other, against the facts. When one turns up that covers all the data available, but does not go beyond any of them, it must be the right one.

The search can be lengthy. We need time to reach good

approximations. When a person understands, he himself grows into that new vision. It is he who knows. In this sense, he has generated an enrichment in his own person; he has created a new expansion of his own personality. Through understanding, a person is evolving, but he is not generating or creating something separate from himself.

When we try to interpret, in modern terms, the ancient belief that man was created to the image of God, we can certainly point to the capacity of man to generate or create understanding—a divine spark in a mortal creature.

results; pressure does not help.

The process we are describing is, of course, not reserved to theologians; it is all too familiar to scientists. They take it for granted that they must test many hypotheses before they can come up with a satisfactory solution. The theologian is on a similar adventure. As scientists are, he too should be left free to formulate hypotheses, but neither the public nor he himself should take the hypotheses as firm judgments about truth.[7]

The correctness of this process rests on two pillars: fidelity to the facts and data available, and creativity in bringing understanding into them. Facts and data come from the outside; we generate the meaning we find in them from the mysterious depths of our own mind.

One can see what an important role the personality of the researcher plays in this process. Without an unbiased mind and detachment from selfish interest, he cannot remain faithful to his data. To make progress towards truth, he must do sustained work. He must be rigorously honest in observing the limits and bounds set by facts. A preconceived idea in him, such as "things must have been the

___

[7]Unfortunately, this is not always the case. In the theologically fertile years after Vatican Council II, especially, many legitimate hypotheses were proposed as final judgments about reality. Quite naturally, the faithful became confused, even to the point of wondering what remained of our faith.

To remedy such a situation, it is often suggested that theological hypotheses should be proposed in a restricted way, for professional theologians only. Nowadays, however, such restriction is impossible. As soon as there is a new insight that could cause sensation or surprise, the communications media will pick it up and spread it far and wide. The remedy should be, rather, in a clear and honest approach to controversial issues by the theologians themselves: if they propose an interesting insight which is not a confirmed hypothesis, they should say so. If they come with a firm judgment, they should demonstrate its truth through the ordinary criteria of theological research.

same all the time," may well ruin the perception of a true change.

Thus, theological prejudice may influence the conclusions. For example, until recently there was a strong trend in writing the history of penance to prove that little change had taken place over the centuries, that confession was present in the same or nearly the same way in the practices of the Mediterranean churches as in the Irish church. It was a judgment that went beyond the evidence we possess.

A Person Reaches True Knowledge When He Surrenders To The Real

The absorption of information, the generation of ideas to express the meaning contained in the data, takes place in our mind. Sooner or later, we must return to the real world and affirm what is truly there, independently from our desires and wishes. To surrender to reality is to go beyond ourselves; it is to accept the world as it is, as God made it, as men have shaped it.[8] Such assent to truth is rightly called "surrender." Our whole person enters into it. We bow humbly before what is, what really exists. There is no true knowledge without humility. Only a humble person can admit his dependence on the real and speak the truth, sweet or bitter as it may be. But such absolute surrender cannot be gratuitous; to be valid it must be critically grounded. Our judgment must be tested in every direction; it must be probed from all sides. Eventually, when we give

---

[8]We are using the term "real" in the ordinary English sense, meaning existing or occurring as fact, "having an objective existence; actually existing as a thing" (OED). In traditional scholastic terminology, "real" can mean, also, something possible but not actually existing, as opposed to something unreal that cannot exist such as a square circle.

our assent to the truth, the right relations are established; we are at peace with ourselves and the world around us.

Yet, let us note immediately, reaching the real is not the same as knowing it fully—perceiving the mountain is not the same as possessing all its secrets. Proclaiming our faith in God's mighty deeds is not the same as entering fully into the vision of his mysteries. Therefore, whenever we reach the truth, our rest must be short. The point of arrival is also a point of departure; there is more to know.

The search for the full truth is, indeed, a never-ending process; it continues as long as there is life in our mind. It is also a self-correcting process. At times, further research brings up new pieces of information and they necessitate revision of all that was understood and judged true. At times, reflection on the process itself reveals that some clues were missed, some unnecessary elements added; therefore, the final judgment must be corrected. Moreover, an examination of the path that our inquiring mind has covered may reveal that we have not been immune from prejudice and bias; then, again, we must revise the results.

We should not be shocked that much of what we know is subject to correction. After all when our mind generates understanding, we are able to comprehend only to a certain degree; nothing is revealed to us in its entirety. Indeed, we are cautiously groping for a better knowledge of things. The process of knowing is an ongoing process which has no limits, since the intimate knowledge which would exhaust all that is contained in this universe is not given to the human mind. Whenever our intelligence comes to rest, there is already a new demand for further progress.

This is how ideas come into being. We are in them; they

are in us. Their roots are in the information that comes from the outside; their being comes from the creative capacity of our mind. Individual judgments are pulled together into well-organized systems of explanation. Through the contribution of many thinkers, there is accumulation of knowledge.

Some Conclusions

Good theology is always informed, intelligent and critically established.[9] If pieces of information are missing, the whole edifice is like the tower of Pisa: it rests on a slanted foundation. But, unlike the tower of Pisa, the theological tower will not remain standing for centuries; it will collapse. If the mind does not see beyond the surface, the understanding will be partial and, consequently, misleading. If the final judgment about the true or false character of a hypothesis has not been critically established, the conclusion will have little to do with reality; it will have a dream-like quality. And when dreams mix with real life, or when a dream is taken for a real event, sooner or later disaster is bound to follow—the tower crumbles.

We can turn our attention, again, to the history of penance and make some applications. The early Mediterranean churches were well aware of the power given to the apostles to forgive sin. But, they did not ask critically enough whether the Lord intended to restrict the use of this power as much as they restricted it. The Irish had an

[9]To avoid any misunderstanding, let us say clearly that we are speaking about the process of reflecting on God's mighty deeds, not about the process of coming to believe in them. Theological reflection starts from the data of revelation. Revelation is accepted through the testimony of the Spirit.

extraordinary insight into the broad scope of that power, but they were less aware of the community dimension of sin and forgiveness. Both perceived something of God's mountain, neither knew it fully. Today, because of our historical perspective, we are in a better position to integrate all known elements into our understanding.

Good theology gives a faithful and precise description of the movement of ideas, even if the search has not produced a final solution. False theology likes to raise an issue in static and sharp alternatives; it looks at everything as being either fully true or entirely false. It treats ideas as monuments, not as living beings.[10]

[10] In other terms, good theology reports on the movement of understanding concerning a point of doctrine. It tries to assess the progress and intensity of that movement. It is not satisfied with a simplistic debate about whether or not a point of doctrine has been defined.

Let us use an illustration. If I know that someone is on a journey to Jerusalem, and I want to know all about the progress of that person, it would not satisfy me to hear that he has not arrived. I want to know how far he has gone, with what speed he is moving, what the prospects are of his arriving.

While the Church is progressing in the understanding of a point of doctrine or the meaning of an institution, it helps little to hear that the matter has not been defined. It does not follow that there is full freedom to believe or not to believe. It does follow, however, that there is a duty for every good member of the believing community to join the search and to reserve judgment on its outcome.

If declarations issued by the ordinary magisterium of the Holy See or the bishops were received in this spirit, we would have fewer problems. Such declarations should be judged as authentic parts of the ongoing movement to understand God's mighty deeds in history and his gifts to the community. Their contributions toward the quest for the full truth should be carefully assessed; they should be balanced and completed by other contributions that may come through the understanding of the faithful at large. Thus, the search can go on. To mount a simplistic defense or opposition often just delays progress.

But, the controversialist spirit of Reformation and Counter Reformation does not die easily. It is marked by thesis pitted against thesis, and hot debate between assenters and dissenters. Such controversies take place, nowadays, mostly within the Catholic Church. They are hardly ever more useful in advancing the cause of understanding than were the debates of the sixteenth century. Rare are, even today, the fine analyses

(2) HOW IDEAS GROW IN LIFE; OR, HOW TRUE DEVELOPMENT CAN BE DISTINGUISHED FROM FALSE GROWTH

If our knowledge of God's own mighty deeds lives and develops, as all living things do, the question arises: how can anyone know what is authentic evolution leading to truth, and what is deceptive change that leads to falsehood?

After all, God's revelation transcends our own knowledge; therefore, its truth or falsity cannot be verified according to our ordinary human criteria. The reality of mysteries is beyond them. The criteria of belief cannot be in historical research or scientific proofs. The ordinary faithful would have no possibility of finding the truth if they had to go through the sophisticated ways of modern scholarship. Yet, Christ has spoken to them; his words were directed to them.[11] He said:

> I bless you, Father, Lord of heaven and of earth, for hiding these things from the learned and the clever and revealing them to mere children (Lk 10:21).

The general answer is that the Church has the Spirit of Christ, has the gift of fidelity in belief and, consequently, can speak the word of God with authenticity. More par-

of developing understanding in the Christian community, analyses that would tell us about the scope, direction and intensity of movement, including reasonable future expectations about its development. And yet, such analyses are what, in the long run, contribute to the increase of our theological knowledge.

[11]When we quote the *logia* of Jesus, we are well aware of the problem of the transmission of his words in the early community. For the purposes of our study, however, the direct way of quoting him, "He said . . . ," is sufficient.

ticularly, we Catholics (and some other Christian churches, too) believe that, in case of conflicting views, through the ministry of the consecrated episcopate, the community has the ultimate power to discern those ideas which are the authentic developments of the understanding of the word of God, and to identify those that are corruptions of it. While the gift of fidelity resides in the whole Church permanently, it is granted to the bishops' college to speak the word with a particular authenticity, especially in times of crisis.

Our Catholic belief is that ecumenical councils have the capacity, in the strength of the Spirit, to determine what is genuine Christian tradition and what is not. Therefore, when an ecumenical council speaks with its full authority, it puts the seal of authenticity on the meaning of human speech that tells us about God's mighty deeds. Vatican Councils I and II stated explicitly what was already known implicitly, that the head of the episcopal body, the Pope, can speak in the name of all, and when he does so, invoking his supreme authority, the same gift of fidelity to the word of God is granted to him as to the whole Church or to the whole college of bishops. He cannot mislead the community.[12]

Such authentication is not an isolated act by which some obscure point of doctrine is suddenly defined. It is usually

---

[12]This fidelity is due to the assistance of the Spirit.
  We wish that Vatican Councils I and II had defined the charism of infallibility in terms of fidelity to God's word. The positive expression says much better what the negative word intends to cover. Many misunderstandings could have been avoided and the intrinsic cohesion of the charism better revealed. As long as the meaning intended by the two councils is retained, there is no reason why we could not present the gift of infallibility as the gift of fidelity to God's revealed word.

the fruit of a long process, a fruit that takes time to mature and contains the seed for future growth.[13] When it happens our response must be intelligent obedience in faith.

But, such obedience is not without its problems. We should respect authority established by God. But it is not always easy to know how far a point of doctrine has received the support of authority.

The following rule, with two practical consequences, may be of some help in recognizing an act of authentic teaching.

Obedience In Faith

The fundamental rule is: *give respect to an act of authority, but precisely as far as there is authority in the act.*[14] The basic assumption behind the rule is simple. Those who have authority in the Church exercise it at different levels. Their act may be a definite pronouncement on some issue; it may be a practical norm

[13]An insightful analysis of this long process is found in Peter Chirico's study, *Infallibility* (Kansas City: Sheed Andrews and McMeel, 1977). He calls infallibility "the crossroads of doctrine." In our judgment, his book is the best reflective contribution, among those that have appeared in recent years, on this issue.

[14]Here we are speaking of teaching authority in the Church as exercised by the pope and the bishops. Obviously, there are other authorities binding the faithful: the Spirit of Christ present to the community, the word of God guiding and shaping the community. The question of how to obey all and each of these authorities is a complex one that we cannot answer here. Let us just say that while every believer owes obedience to the Spirit, to interpret his inspiration authentically is not given to everyone. While the word of God binds every person in the community, its authentic interpretation is a difficult process. Conflicts do arise; they are simply unavoidable when mortal beings wrestle with the understanding of God's mysteries. Often enough, conflicts are like labor pains; eventually they bring forth new life in the Church.

for the sake of good government; it may be an exhortation, and so forth. Our attitude should be a response to their intention, neither more nor less.

There are two consequences. *Do not downgrade authority. Do not upgrade authority.*

To downgrade authority means not to acknowledge a power that is there in the act to bind us in the name of the Lord or by the strength of the Spirit. A Christian would be guilty of such an attitude if, for instance, he treated the Nicean Creed, which is a profession of faith, as a pious exhortation; or if he regarded a solemn proclamation issued by the Pope about Christian doctrine as a pious exhortation. To downgrade authority is to ignore it, to deny it or, in some extreme cases, to show downright contempt for it.

To upgrade authority means to attribute more weight to official pronouncements and acts than has been given to them by those who issued them. A Christian would be guilty of such intemperate conduct if he believed that every statement in the documents of Vatican Council II is a formal definition; or, if he took an obviously occasional homily by the Pope as deciding a point of faith; or, if he treated an instruction issued by a Roman Congregation, without a special mandate from the Pope, as if it were legislation for the universal Church. To upgrade authority is to attempt to be wiser than the Church, to give an assent that is not asked for.

While malice in downgrading authority is easily recognized, the upgrading of authority is sometimes presented as a virtue. For some strange reason it is assumed that if someone regards a non-infallible pronouncement as infallible, he is more loyal to the Church than someone who tries to give the proper respect due in the circumstances. His faith is stronger! Such a proposition is a flagrant fallacy. Anyone who upgrades authority fails on two counts: he gives an assent of faith when it is not due, and he does not use his critical intelligence when he should.

As the downgrading of authority can cause fragmentation in the community, so the upgrading of it can lead to serious breakdowns. To give more value to a pronouncement than is due is a deviation from truth; it is a surrender to falsehood. But, falsehood has no lasting value. One day the reckoning is bound to come, and it does—when truth is discovered. Then the result is shock and trauma, often followed by a crisis of faith. No wonder! An act of faith has been asked for, or given, when it was not warranted. Much of the post-Vatican II crisis among the faithful was caused by earlier upgrading of beliefs by well-meaning writers and preachers. In the aftermath of the Council, when many myths and much misplaced piety were swept away, many Catholics thought that their faith was under attack—in danger of being destroyed!

Those in pastoral work, especially preachers and teachers, should be careful not to mislead the people either by downgrading or upgrading authority. Loyalty to the Pope and bishops means that exactly the same weight should be given to a statement or ordinance as they put into it. They know only too well with how much authority they want to act in a given case. To attribute either more or less weight to their words or actions than they freely choose to grant them is false loyalty, and disservice to the Church.

(3) WHAT AUTHENTIC AND INAUTHENTIC DEVELOPMENT IS; OR, A SHORT DISCOURSE ON CRITICAL AND UNCRITICAL METHOD

Good theology is always based on critical method.

Dogmatic theology has benefited for a long time from a critical method that was not entirely missing even when theology was suffering from a lack of intellectual vigor. It was not so in the field of moral theology. In fact, the developments of these two branches of theology can serve as examples of critical and uncritical development, of controlled and uncontrolled evolution.

There was controlled growth in dogmatic theology. Ecumenical councils exercised a strong critical function and judged the authenticity of doctrine, especially before the Eastern schism took place. More often than not, the process was dialectical: questions arose about some points of Christian tradition and different groups presented different answers. The bishops, assembled in council, accepted one of the positions as orthodox; that is, they saw the meaning of the Scriptures unfolding in it. They rejected the other positions as unorthodox, as being "against the Scriptures."

From the early Middle Ages onwards, the course of critically controlled development in understanding the mysteries of our faith was promoted by the development of the so-called "qualifications." They were short statements that determined the grade of certainty with which propositions concerning the revelation were to be held.

Many who studied theology before Vatican Council II remember how each thesis in dogma had to be "qualified," that is, its binding force had to be determined with precision. Some theses were articles of faith, *de fide definita*; some were close to being defined as such, *fidei proxima*; some merely stated the common opinion of theologians, *opinio communis theologorum*. Their respective contraries were heresy, *opinio haeretica*; or, a view close to heresy, *haeresi proxima*; or, a proposition offensive to pious ears, *piis auribus offensiva*. Admittedly, the owner of those pious ears was never identified!

Two main factors contributed to the development of the system of qualifications. One was the practical need to know where orthodoxy ended and heresy began, so that the unity of faith in the community could be safeguarded; it was mostly a pastoral task exercised by synods and councils. The other was the development of the scientific approach to the doing of theology. There was the need to assess the grade of our knowledge of the mysteries; this was primarily an intellectual task performed by theologians. The two needs, to identify heresy where it existed and to have a better idea of the content of faith, went side by side and were complementary to each other. The fact stands that there was an insistence, in the Church, on critically evaluating the importance of every theological statement. It assured that the development of doctrine was controlled—to a point, anyway. Arguments were not always sound, nor was there much sensitivity for progress; nonetheless, there was an awareness that strict proof was needed before a proposition could be called an article of faith or its opposite condemned as heresy. It was a sound enough rule in an otherwise objectionable system.[15]

[15]Among the agents that promoted the critically controlled development of dogmatic theology were the tribunals of the Inquisition. When someone was accused of doctrinal deviation the court had to determine the

After the Council of Trent, as the teaching of theology through the "thesis" system emerged, the elements of the earlier "critical method" survived and even flourished in universities and seminaries. Teachers and students had to "qualify" their theses, and they had to prove the correctness of their "qualifications" from primary sources: from the Scriptures, from the Fathers, from councils, and from other witnesses of our traditions. Many of their proofs would not stand examination today. Nonetheless, an effort was made to be selective and critical, even if the tools of critical thinking were not well-developed.

Also, it is a historical fact that the bishops, throughout the centuries, paid more attention to dogmatic theology than to many other matters. From Nicea to Vatican II, they exercised a fairly strict control over its development.

The opposite example, of uncontrolled and uncritical growth, can be found in moral theology, especially as it developed between the Council of Trent and Vatican Council II. Obviously, we are speaking of a prevailing trend, in no

charge, but this could not be done without assessing the quality or binding force of a point of doctrine that was denied or doubted by the accused. The court employed theologians to perform this task. By determining the doctrinal weight of a proposition they really set the charge.

Allowing for many historical variations, in general it can be said that the qualifications were important for the tribunals of Inquisition because, as a rule, the gravity of the crime and the severity of the punishment depended on them. If a person was found guilty of heresy there were times when his life was in jeopardy. If he was convicted as "suspect of heresy," he was likely to escape with a lighter sentence. If he was found as holding something against the common opinion of theologians, the judges might have thought of him as a fellow lacking in learning or intelligence, even as dangerous, but they could not excommunicate him. In a judicial system that could be cruel there was a principle of justice: no one should be exposed to the extreme rigor of the law unless it was certain beyond any doubt that he was guilty of heresy. (Cf. *Dictionnaire de théologie catholique*, vol. 7, 2016-2068; *Lexikon fuer Theologie und Kirche*, vol. 5, 698-702).

way indicting every individual writer. There were exceptions. We ourselves studied moral theology before Vatican II and received excellent training in it.

Yet, anyone looking at moral theology textbooks of a pre-Vatican II vintage is bound to notice in many of them a certain absence of critical thinking. There are few references to scriptural, patristic or conciliar sources; there are many "deductions" from "theological principles." There is little effort to "qualify" an affirmation critically. Statements are presented as true on the basis of the "common opinion of moral theologians" whose authority is often upgraded beyond sound measure. Solutions are proposed that certainly look absurd to the uninitiated.[16] Practices are encouraged that could subtly match, or outdo, the severity of the Inquisition.

For instance, the tribunals of the Inquisition, as a matter

[16]We recall one case, found in some of those books, that for us remains forever the classical example of how absurd uncritical casuistry can get. The case concerns Peter who decides to kill his enemy Paul. Peter, waiting in the dark for Paul, notices someone coming. He assumes that it is Paul and promptly strikes down his enemy. On closer inspection, he discovers that, by mistake, he killed John. John was the breadwinner for a large family; his wife and ten children are now destitute. The question is, "Does Peter owe anything to the family of John?" The answer is, "Probably not." He never intended to kill John, it was a mere accident. The fact that Peter intended to strike down a living human person, no matter whether it was Paul or John, and that he committed a crime which cries to heaven, was not enough to bind him morally to support the family, which remained without help.

Of course not all authors have proceeded in this way. But we still recall a student, taking his comprehensive examination in moral theology, who desperately defended Peter's immunity from any compensation, over against our objections; and this was just about ten years ago.

It is never fair to judge an intellectual movement by the occasional aberrations that are bound to occur, yet some absurdities may point to serious deficiencies in method and mentality.

of principle,[17] did not excommunicate anybody from the visible Church for the sin of heresy, unless they found proofs from Christian tradition, and proofs beyond any doubt, that the person was guilty of denying an article of faith. Moral theologians, however, often determined what was a mortal sin on no stronger evidence than their own common opinion. Then priests, in confessional practice, told ordinary Christians that they would not be absolved unless they followed the opinion of theologians. In this subtle way, a new form of "excommunication" arose: people were not excluded from the visible Church, but they were told that there was no reconciliation for them unless they obeyed.

A lack of attentiveness, an absence of critical insights, a deficiency of controlled rational judgments, eventually brought corresponding results: a system of thought emerged and was imposed on the consciousness of the faithful not so much by genuine teaching authority as by some teachers in universities, seminaries, and other schools. It was widely believed and said that, on the opinion of theologians, provided they were sufficient in numbers, the quality and gravity of a sin could be established with such firmness that all priests had the duty to apply the doctrine in their confessional practice. In this way, moral theologians unwittingly, and even unwillingly, became arbiters of eternal life and death, of salvation and damnation. Their "sentences" were readily and steadily imposed on the faithful in the confessionals. Those who did not promise to obey were denied absolution.

[17]Let us stress this: we speak of a matter of principle, not of what happened here and there in practice. The trial and condemnation of Joan of Arc certainly did not uphold any lofty principle!

In reality, such theologians never received a mandate from the Lord, or the Church, to pronounce about eternal, or even temporal, life or death. They had no doctrinal authority. Infallibility could never be delegated, and even if such delegation had been possible, there is no evidence that it ever existed in their favor.

Such assumption of authority provoked questions, but they were answered in a perfunctory way. It was asserted that in moral theology it was not possible to use conventional "proofs" similar to those used in dogmatic theology. There was no need to examine the Scriptures, to look into conciliar and other authentic sources of our traditions. The Scriptures did not contain a systematic doctrine of morality, and the Church hardly ever spoke on such matters—so people were told. Hence, the only existing authority was that of the moral theologians; their opinions should be accepted as reflecting the mind of the Church.

This is, of course, a classical case of exercising authority by self-delegation with no authorization. No wonder that the manual-type moral theology is shaken to its very foundations today. A good part of it was not built on a rock; much of it was not authentic development of the traditions of the Church. If ever renewal means return to the sources, it does so in the case of the renewal of moral theology.

There is another problem, too: the invasion of the Christian conscience by an exaggerated theology of sin. Ancient practices that sprang from devotion, such as the observance of Sunday, the practice of fasting and abstinence, the saying of the divine office by diocesan and regular clergy, all were caught in the net of legal duties binding under pain of mortal sin.[18] The shift from voluntary offerings to grave obligations eventually led to the creation of a bad situation. Overburdened by the possibility of sin from every side, sheer common sense prompted the Christians to look for escape. Therefore, a mentality evolved that assumed that whenever there was no obligation under mortal sin, there was no obligation at all. There was, in the community, a longing for the freedom of the children of God; hence, everybody chose freedom whenever there was no threat of hell. Now and again, authorities became apprehensive of loopholes and, to close them, they imposed even more obligations under pain of sin. People responded according to their mentality and, with the connivance of

---

[18]We have two observations concerning the transformation of free devotional observances into gravely binding legal duties.

First, we are not convinced that the imposition of an observance by law, under pain of "mortal sin," really makes people more fervent or even more observant. Let me recall an experience from my own childhood. I grew up in a small town in Hungary. Half of the population was Catholic, half was Protestant. We happened to live in a house that was close to both the Catholic and Protestant churches. It was easy to observe the crowds that came to the services on Sundays. They were usually of the same size. The question came into my mind, and I was a child, "How is it that the number of those who go to church on Sunday is about the same on both sides, although Catholics 'sin mortally' if they do not go, and Protestants do not?"

We think that, if the insistence on legal obligations ceased, there might be some transitional oscillation in the number of those who attend Mass on Sunday, but eventually we would settle down to more or less the same numbers attending as we have now.

Second, the legislator most certainly can say that he intends to bind the consciences of the faithful, and gravely so. However, ordinarily it is not the intention of the legislator, even if the Pope is legislating himself, to make a doctrinal pronouncement, through the text of the law, about the precise gravity of the sin concerned. Therefore, ordinarily again, the most the legislator should say is that he intends to impose a grave obligation. Then it should be left to theologians to work out what that means in the broader doctrinal context of moral theology. At any rate, we think that, as a rule, duties concerning worship and devotion should be considered proper matters for pastoral care, and not for legislation.

benign moral theologians, invented even more distinctions to free themselves from an often impossible burden. Such a vicious circle led to the erosion of both the healthy fear of sin and the simple generosity that wants to offer joyful sacrifices to the Lord.

For all this, we are paying the price today. It is enough to say that a given practice, e.g. being present at Mass on Sundays, is not binding under mortal sin to hear the response: "Then, I am not bound to go!" As if anyone could be a good Christian without wanting to worship with his community! To repair such erosion of generosity will take the effort of several generations. Nothing is so difficult as to change the human mind.

But, the task we are facing is not impossible. We have ample resources in God's Spirit—and our own human intelligence. Also, there are plenty of sources in Christian tradition to inspire a new moral theology built on better foundations.

Conclusion

There are many studies tracing the development of the sacrament of penance as an institution. Also, there are numerous studies describing the evolution of the understanding of Christian morality throughout the centuries. There has been less effort among historians and theologians to examine their mutual relationship, to assess the impact of the institution of penance on moral doctrine and, vice versa, to evaluate the influence of moral theology on the administration of the sacrament.

There is a close connection between the two. The relatively restrained use of public penance was compatible only with an understanding that relatively few Christians sin so gravely that their friendship with God and their relationship with the community is broken, and that they do so rarely. There was a balance, a proportion, between the conception of sin and the process of forgiving.

The highly expanded views of private penance introduced by the Irish opened the door for a new theology of sin which found mortal gravity in many actions where it was not discovered before, and found it easy to impose an absolute duty to confess them. The massive volumes of penitential books in the hand of the priest took the place of the slender lists of sins that once were kept in the Mediterranean churches. There was a new balance between the conception of sin and the process of forgiving.

The confessional practice that was sanctioned by Lateran Council IV, and received a new impetus from the Council of Trent, depended heavily on the doctrine of moralists who, in many cases, required confession and absolution to obtain the forgiveness of sins. Their teaching was imposed on the faithful with such thoroughness that no one could escape it.

If we are looking into the future, that is, into the institutional reform of the sacrament of penance and the rethinking of Christian teaching about morality, we must be aware that one cannot be done without the other. The use of the sacrament is, to a large extent, determined by those who can speak with some authority about the conditions of grace and sin, about life and death in God's kingdom.

The future development of the sacrament of penance will depend much on the evolution of moral theology.

3

Third Question about Persons: How Do They Change?

We are continuing our journey. First, we looked at external events; then we reflected on the living insights and judgments behind them; now, we look at ourselves, living persons as we are. We are trying to understand the changes that take place not in outside events, not in the content of our developing ideas, but in us, inside us. We are trying to understand how we change. In doing so, we should be on the alert. As a rule we are intent on looking outward. We assume that change happens outside only, or in the realm of ideas only; we are rarely aware that its source is in ourselves.

Indeed, the history of discoveries shows that it has been easier for man to look outwards than to turn inwards. Astronomy was one of the first sciences to develop: Claudius Ptolemy built up his theory of the heavens around 150 A.D. Depth psychology was among the last: Sigmund Freud published his work on the interpretation of dreams, *Die Traumdeutung,* in 1900.

Often enough we behave like a person traveling on a train who has just been awakened from his slumber—he opens his eyes and sees how the whole world is moving rapidly by; he feels that he is the only steady point in the universal flow.

Changing Man and Changing Society

We are indeed traveling in time, we are part of an historical universe. We are not fixed monuments surrounded by movements. We cannot look at anything from an immovable platform. All our judgments about external changes must take into account changes in ourselves or, better still, our changing selves.

We are historical beings; we live in time, we cannot step outside it. We cannot take an absolute measurement of the flow of events from a fixed position; we are part of the universal movement that penetrates the whole created world. For this reason, we are able to shape history, but we are also shaped by it.

We are really stressing the obvious: we, too, are subject to the law of life in this universe. Life means movement; lack of movement spells death. As long as we live, we move. The present is no more than a point of passage into the future.

Therefore, when a person looks at the flow of external events or reflects on changing ideas, he should be aware that he himself is moving, too. He perceives outside happenings, generates insights and formulates judgments from his own particular moving position and disposition. He cannot do anything else without going out of this world.[1]

It follows that all his descriptions of the events that pass by him with lesser or greater rapidity, all his interpretations of the meaning of those events, are given from his

[1] A cognitional theory which includes the transmission of knowledge through universal concepts may lead easily to a tacit assumption that we can place ourselves outside of the flow of history. After all, once the essence of an object has been grasped and expressed in a "spiritual" way, in the form of a universal concept, that comprehension endures and is able to resist the vicissitudes of history. Moreover, with proper care it can be handed over from generation to generation; hence the saying, *semper idem,* "always the same."

In reality, knowledge is not that uniform or standardized. A meaning is created by every comprehending person on the basis of the information that has reached him. The capacity of the living person to assimilate information, to understand it, to subject his own insight to critical evaluation, enters into the process of knowing. Therefore, all knowledge is, in some way, individual and historically conditioned. There is simply no other type of knowledge available to mortal man.

own moving standpoint; they bear the mark of his own changing self.

To achieve objectivity in describing any event, this moving standpoint, this "change-full" nature, of the human person must be taken into account. A true report on any event takes into account not only the external data but also both the movement of ideas and the ongoing development of persons.

There is no cheap philosophical relativism in this approach. Nor is it Pilate's skepticism, "What is the truth?" On the contrary, it is the discovery of the true relationship between the object and the subject, that is, between the known and the knower. It takes into account the real position of both, and, therefore, leads to a better knowledge of what exists.

Changing Church

Since the Church is a living society it must move. About its movement of life we can be optimistic indeed: in the long run, it is progress. It is a movement toward fulness. The Lord himself promised that those who believed in him would be led by his Spirit into the full truth. Civilizations may rise and fall; empires may march on to the scene of history triumphantly, and exit from it shamefully; the community of believers lives on.

Believers know the vicissitudes of history. They, too, experience triumphant rises and disastrous declines; but, behind it all, there is progress. Such movement can be described as an evolutionary process from point Alpha to Omega; or, it can be illustrated through the metaphor of the seed growing into a tree and bringing forth fruit a hundredfold. No matter how we talk of it, it is progress into a more abundant life.

Such evolution is primarily in the minds and hearts of the faithful. Ideas are conceived there; love is born there.

Whether or not to participate in this process is a question for every Christian, a question that must be answered by each one personally. No one can avoid it, certainly not in our days. The person's decision determines his ongoing relationship to the word of God. He can take it and treasure it as a precious but inanimate object, or he can take it as the living seed destined to bear fruit in his heart.

In this chapter, we want to achieve some understanding of the changing man who is, also, a Christian. When that happens, we shall have a better comprehension of the evolving human community that is the Church. We do not intend, however, to present all the aspects of the development of a person or a community. Rather, we want to call the attention of the reader to the nature of some principal changes so that, once he has read our exposition, he can go on his own tour of discovery.

Our search will not focus on outside events, past, present or future, or on the content of our ideas either. We are interested, now, in human persons, persons who are growing, developing and expanding in their capacity to know. Hence, if the reader wants to follow our exposition, he must turn into himself, and discover his own changing self—that is the person closest to him!

In the following pages, we shall describe five types of movement which can take place in a human person and are likely to affect his perception of the outside world, and of his own internal universe. They are really five aspects of the development of a person. Although we present them as distinct from each other analytically, this does not imply that they are separate from each other. When a botanist describes the growth of a plant, he cannot make himself understood unless he breaks the one life movement into its component elements and gives an explanation of each. But, when he has finished his analysis, he must turn to his audience and deny what he has done. There are no separate movements. All is one, in an all-embracing movement of life.

The five aspects of personal development are as follows:[2]

(1) Every person develops a fundamental attitude toward the world in which he lives—materially and spiritually. He can be a settler in it, and reluctant to move out; or, he can be a pioneer, wanting to explore what is beyond it. He can move from one attitude to the other.

(2) A person can be of classical mind, that is he can conceive of himself as standing at an immovable point in this universe from where all events, all thoughts can be known with an absolute exactness that remains valid forever; or, he can be of historical mind, that is he can be aware that he himself is part of a historical process that allows him to grow closer to the truth, but hardly ever to possess it in its fulness. A person can move from classical to historical mentality.

(3) Every person sees as far as his horizon allows. It may be limited to the immediate neighborhood, or it may reach

[2]We would like to request that, after each point, the reader ask himself, "Does my internal experience confirm what I have read?" If his answer is, "Yes," the communication between the writer and the reader is alive and working well. If it is, "No," there is a whole new field for his exploration: what are the reasons for different experiences?

óut far and wide to include fields and objects that are at a great distance. A person can expand his capacity to see, and move into new horizons.

(4) The specific standpoint of a person determines his angle of vision and his particular perception. He can mistakenly think that he sees everything around when, in fact, he sees only a segment of the universe. He must be dislodged from his position to have a more comprehensive perception of reality.

(5) Finally, every human person trying to understand the world around him, and in him, operates with some categories of perception. They help him to bring order, cohesion and harmony into the disparate data perceived by his senses. But categories are human creations; they can be crude and simple, or sophisticated and complex. A person changes through the development of his mental categories.

We will take these aspects in turn. At times we shall speak through parables, at times through abstract concepts. One approach should complete and balance the other.

(1) THE PARABLE OF THE TWO CHARACTERS: THE SETTLER AND THE PIONEER

Every person develops a fundamental attitude toward the world in which he lives—materially and spiritually. He can be a settler in it, and reluctant to move out; or, he can be a pioneer, wanting to explore what is beyond it. He can move from one attitude to the other.

Once upon a time there lived two persons in the same valley, one was a settler, the other a pioneer. The settler found the valley comfortable and friendly; he made his dwelling in it. He developed great familiarity with the surrounding countryside, with the fields and brooks, with the forests and the mountains. He had no desire to find new countries inhabited by people speaking strange languages. He had no desire to find the source of the river, nor had he any wish to follow its course to find the far-away ocean; still less had he thought of ever boarding a ship, so precariously balanced on top of the water.

The settler knew his surroundings well. He was not in the habit of raising questions about them; his life was not a search for answers. Of course, he experienced disturbing moments, such as when a traveler came through and spoke about new methods of agriculture elsewhere; the tale made him uncomfortable. At times, he did not believe it; at times, he did not want to hear it.

He knew all the questions that could be raised about the valley, and he knew all the answers. He was born in the valley; there he intended to die.

The pioneer lived in the valley too, and learned to know it as well as the settler. He, too, heard the strange tales coming from beyond the mountains; he, too, experienced disturbing questions. But, unlike the settler, he listened.

He wanted to know where the river came from; he wished to explore its source. He wanted to see where it went to; he wished to follow its course to the ocean.

He grew interested in new methods of agriculture; he was determined to try them out.

To fulfill his dreams and desires, the pioneer went out of the valley often enough; he went to explore the world that lay beyond the snow-covered mountains.

Settler and pioneer: the one stays in the valley, the other

goes to explore the world. What makes them so different from each other? Not the external universe, both see the same. Not the questions alone, both hear them all. The difference is deeper; it is in their mentality. Let us look at them closer.

The settler may be a good man, but he does not carry forward any cause, be it for the better or for the worse. He lets the world go by; he gives little to it, and does not ask for much in exchange.

To understand him even better, let us recall an experience common to us all.

When we were small and in grade school, we were taught about the multiplication table. It was a self-contained world where all the figures were neatly ordered. Slowly, we took possession of that world, we mastered it, inside-out. We were fascinated by its simplicity and clarity. We learned its laws and lived by them; they brought us success and recognition. We knew all the questions that could be raised, and the answers were at our fingertips. We were secure.

Of course, we were aware that the maneuvers could be extended well beyond ten-by-ten, but that caused no worry. All the questions were predictable, all the answers available. No more was needed than a larger multiplication table.

The settler is a person who lives contented within a small universe, not unlike a child whose happy world is circumscribed by the multiplication table. In such a world all goes well as long as all questions move within the pre-set framework. But the very foundations of that world can be shaken when someone begins to raise seemingly absurd issues. What happens if three is deducted from two? Or five is divided by seven? Instantly a person, who is in full possession of the clarity and security that only the world of the multiplication table can give, is disturbed. What should he make of such nonsense? There are no answers to those questions! Intinctively, the settler turns away from the issue.

He may call the questions silly. He may brand the questioner ignorant, troublesome, or even rebellious. Or, he may simply not listen. If he has power, he may try to silence the inquirer.

For the settler, even to recognize the questions as valid would mean to go out of his own little world into the unknown. Such a decision would affect his whole being, his mind, his health, his emotions, his soul, his body, all.

To be converted from a settler into a pioneer means to accept good questions and to move into the unknown to search for the answers. Such a decision reaches every fiber of a person.

The pioneer is the one who is open to questions.[3] He can

---

[3]Kenneth Clark, in his *Civilisation,* gives a splendid description of an explorer:

In the autumn of 1513, soon after the death of Julius, there arrived, to stay in the Belvedere of the Vatican, one more giant—Leonardo da Vinci. Historians used to speak of him as a typical Renaissance man. This is a mistake. If Leonardo belongs in any epoch it is in the later seventeenth century; but in fact he belongs to no epoch, he fits into no category, and the more you know about him, the more mysterious he becomes. Of course, he had certain Renaissance characteristics. He loved beauty and graceful movement . . .

But all these gifts were dominated by one ruling passion which was not a Renaissance characteristic—curiosity. He was the most relentlessly curious man in history. Everything he saw made him ask why and how. Why does one find sea-shells in the mountains? How do they build locks in Flanders? How does a bird fly? What accounts for cracks in walls? What is the origin of wind and clouds? How does one stream of water deflect another? Find out; write it down; if you can see it, draw it. Copy it out. Ask the same live with the uncertainty they bring, provided, of course, they are good questions. He can take risks. He can move into the unknown. Certainly, a promising adventure may end in a fiasco; then the explorer has no choice but to retrace his steps back to the valley, and start all over again. Yet, a disturbing question may also lead into a new universe. It may lead from elementary mathematics to the discovery of the worlds of negative numbers, irrational numbers, imaginary numbers, complex numbers, and so on, to no end.

Penance

Among the protagonists in the history of the sacrament of penance we find both settlers and pioneers.

In the beginning all had to be pioneers. The Lord gave power to the apostles to forgive sins, but he did not determine any procedure that they had to follow. He gave them his Spirit to guide them, that was enough. Indeed, the early communities around the Mediterranean had to create their own ritual for the forgiveness of sins.

Later, the Irish, in their way, went through the same process. They knew about the mysterious power to forgive, and, as Christians of earlier generations, they too felt free to create the signs of pardon. There was one forgiveness of sins in the Church, as there was one baptism, but, after Christianity penetrated into Ireland and the Church came

question again and again and again. Leonardo's curiosity was matched by an incredible mental energy. Reading the thousands of words in Leonardo's notebooks, one is absolutely worn out by this energy. He won't take yes for an answer. He can't leave anything alone—he worries it, re-states it, answers imaginary antagonists (pp. 133-135).

to life there, there were definitely two distinct patterns to signify it.

The bishops of the Council of Toledo (589), who forbade the introduction of a new rite and insisted on the old discipline right down to its extreme severity, had the mind of settlers. It is inconceivable that they should not have heard some good questions such as, why did so few of the faithful do penance? or, why was it necessary to do it publicly? etc. Yet, they had only one answer: they decreed that the old discipline had to be followed.

The bishops of Chalon (644-656) were pioneers for their own times. They heard the questions: should the process of forgiveness be open to all? or, should it be reserved for a few who wanted to become penitents? They must have felt the danger of forgetting the gravity of sin, of making life all too easy, yet they moved out into the unknown and declared that penance is a remedy for the soul, and, therefore, should be open to all.

The period of conflict that followed, for some five centuries, was not just a discussion about authentic traditions and legitimate innovations. It was a conflict of mentalities as well, even if the protagonists did not know it. The Carolingian reformers were set to restore the old, with little openness for anything new. The movement that eroded their attempt at restoration, and led to the final approval of auricular confession at Lateran Council IV (1215), was a movement of relentless questions which were answered not so much by theoretical statements as by practical decisions.

Let the matter rest here, even if there are more examples of settlers and pioneers in the later history of this sacrament. For the moment, enough has been said to illustrate the importance of change in such fundamental attitudes.

Moral Theology

There is hardly any need to point out that among those who cultivated moral theology there were always settlers and pioneers. The settlers wanted to remain within the framework of the system that was handed over to them; they spent much of their energy defending and perfecting it. Pioneers moved out to find new depths in Christian teaching.

The mentality of the settler manifested itself, especially in recent centuries, in the somewhat uncritical reliance of many moral theologians on various authorities. Some were all too much inclined to upgrade the authority of official pronouncements by the Church, giving more weight to them than what was due by the sound criteria of our faith. Some went even further and followed all too slavishly the opinions of theologians who preceded them, especially when such masters had achieved a certain reputation. The search for new light in the primary sources of our tradition did not go side by side with respect for authorities.

Since there was little fresh input from early and original sources, since there was little critical revision of studies transmitted from generation to generation, a strongly traditional attitude, that at times amounted to intellectual stagnation, was bound to follow. Writers tended to preserve what was approved by authorities, whether in official pronouncements or in the books of approved theologians. Little progress was made over long periods of time.

The picture today is a mixed one. There are certainly many genuine pioneers around, who find fresh inspiration in the Scriptures, in the Fathers, in the life of Christian communities through the centuries. They feel challenged by new questions. With the hesitation, caution, and self-criticism that characterize all genuine research, they are able to point toward new solutions, even if they are slow to defend any of them as final.

At the same time, there are those in the field of moral theology who keep the mentality of the settler but speak the language of the pioneer. When they propose new solutions, they do not do so on the basis of critical research; rather, they advocate them relying on new and dubious authorities, such as popular movements, theological fashions, mere empirical research, and so forth. They are settlers, and they do not even know it! Unfortunately, they can easily deceive the faithful.

Confusing as our times can be, they are God's times. The kingdom of God is like a field where the master has sown the good seed, and some enemy the bad one; they grow side by side. It was ever thus, from the beginning; it is so today. But whenever the days of harvesting came, and there were many in our history, the Church, led by the Spirit of Christ, was always able to discern the wheat from the chaff, and to keep the wheat in its barns.

(2) THE PROGRESS FROM SYSTEMATIC VISION OF PERFECTION TO ONGOING AND SELF-CORRECTING UNDERSTANDING; OR, FROM CLASSICAL TO HISTORICAL MENTALITY

A person can be of classical mind, that is he can conceive of himself as standing at an immovable point in this universe, from where all events, all thoughts can be known with an absolute exactness that remains

*valid forever; or, he can be of historical mind, that is
he can be aware that he himself is part of a historical
process that allows him to grow closer to the truth,
but hardly ever to possess it in its fulness. A person
can move from classical to historical mentality.*

The great scholastic systems of theology have been compared to Gothic cathedrals, and not without good
reasons. Not only were they construed at the same time;
there was also a similarity in their internal structures. The
builders of high-soaring cathedrals used their stones with
meticulous precision. In the unity of the whole edifice,
they balanced them so finely that the integrity of the whole
depended on each stone having the right shape and staying
at the right place. To take away one would have caused the
edifice to collapse. Theological systems were conceived
with ideas chiseled to no less exacting measures than stones
used for houses of worship, and their internal balance was
not less precarious than that of the soaring arches.

As we well know, cathedrals do not grow, they remain
the same; there is no life in stones. Systems of thought
built with similar elements do not grow easily, either; they
tend to remain monuments to be admired forever. Stone
buildings, beautiful as they look, closed systems of
thought, fascinating as they are, have no life in them. They
are not like seed sown in good soil. They do not grow.

As a new age dawned on us under the impact of the
development of empirical sciences, even more under the influence of philosophical reflections that turned to the internal world of man, the great conceptual systems were
called into question. In particular, their component
elements, the well-defined essences expressed in universal

concepts, were less and less accepted.

The world moved away from what is known as classical mentality toward a new understanding of the universe.

In recent theological writings much has been said about this development: the progress from classical to historical mentality. The theme is important. Without grasping the basic difference between the two, much that has happened in modern theology cannot be adequately undertood; in particular, the evolutionary nature of our knowledge cannot be appreciated.

Let us say, therefore, a few explanatory words. Our intention is not to give a full description of the two mentalities, only to give some guidance to recognize them—even when they appear in disguise, as they often do.

To know the "classical mentality" we should go to Athens and contemplate the Parthenon, a building of perfect proportions, standing there immutable under the blue Greek sky, majestic even in its ruins. There is a perfection in that building, a perfection that represents the ideal order in nature which cannot be improved on.

Indeed, a person of classical mentality believes that there is a perfection in nature, there is an ideal order in the universe, that can be discovered and known without distortion. Once found, man can take possession of it, he can reproduce it. When he has done so, his efforts come to an end. There is nothing beyond perfection to discover, to know, and to build.

Such a mentality was not confined to ancient Greece. The Romans believed in the *pax Romana,* an ideal order, a harmonious balance among all the members of the empire. Once established, it was there to stay.

The belief in immutable beauty and harmony accessible

to man leads the person of classical mentality to a strong fundamental attitude. He believes in search and progress—up to a point. That point is "perfection." Once the ideal order is discovered, his principal virtues are stability and fidelity. For him, a proposal for any significant change is a threat; change can only be for the worse. It would destroy order and beauty. Some small developments may be useful accidentally, but never in substance. After all, how could anyone improve on what is perfect! Logically enough, change and movement is looked at with suspicion. Structures once built must stand—forever. Like the Parthenon.

The person who is of the "historical mentality" builds his life and outlook on a different assumption. He believes that he himself, his whole being, is part of a great movement that makes up our history. While he moves, he has a few small windows to look out at his surroundings, like someone who is flying in a plane and watches the earthly objects roll by.

Obviously, information is pouring in through the small windows, the windows in this case being our senses. But what reaches us is only a small part of all that can be seen, grasped, and assimilated. Yet, out of these fragments we must constitute our universe. We know that there is much beyond, but we must work with the limited data available. To gain more knowledge, we steadily reach out for more information and for a better understanding of it all. Thus, our life is an unending process of knowing, and wanting to know, more. We never come to a perfect halt. The process is not completed, ever.

Such an historical approach to learning generates, again, a fundamental attitude: a commitment to movement. Since to increase our knowledge means to have more information and to reflect on it with greater intensity, we must be engaged in a steady search that brings us closer to the fulness of truth. To think in evolutionary terms becomes a way of life. Movement is not imperfection, it is needed to reach a more perfect knowledge. Succeeding discoveries and reflections do affect our earlier judgments either by compelling us to reverse them, or to correct them, or to reaffirm them with greater strength. We do not reject ultimate perfection, but we conceive of ourselves as being on the way towards it, with places to rest here and there, never quite arriving in this life.

Stability and fidelity are still considered virtues but with a difference: the pilgrim must keep the goal of his journey steadily in mind, and continue his progress faithfully.

It would be wrong to assume, though, that a person of historical mentality is not interested in truth. On the contrary, his quest for the whole truth is the moving force of his life. But he realizes that he comes into the possession of truth slowly and painfully, step by step.

Transition in the Church

For many centuries, beginning with the age of Scholasticism, theology found a comforting home with the classical mentality. Once truth was discovered, the search came to an end. The researchers could rest. No serious change was necessary, indeed conceivable. In many ways the same mentality has been imprinted on the Catholic community.

It is clear that we must move away from the classical

outlook but it is not easy to acquire the historical mentality. It is not a transition from one conceptual system to another, as is sometimes mistakenly assumed. It is not merely the study of more history, either. It is much more: it is a change in the person. He must see and understand himself differently: he must perceive his whole being as part of the historical universe; he must know himself as a constantly developing individual.

No wonder that, even today, many theologians are ill-at-ease with the historical mentality, or pay lip-service to it while steadily living by the classical one. They fear that by stressing the continuous flow of things and ideas, the permanence of truth is jeopardized. Yet, it is not so.

The role of the Church witnessing the truth is precisely to say that there are arrivals, even if every point of arrival becomes a point of departure in the process. But when a fragment of truth is found, it must not be lost any more. The Council of Nicea in 325 sealed the truth that the Father and the Son are of the same substance, that is, that they are distinct in their personhood but equal in their divinity. No further development can cancel out or ignore such an acquisition of the truth, authenticated by the Spirit through a council. Yet, the truth of Nicea did not say, once for all, everything that we can ever know about the Trinity; rather, by saying so little it inspired the Church to progress further in the understanding of this mystery. A point of arrival became a point of departure. More examples could be given, but the pattern of explanation remains the same.

Today, we are in a period of transition. Both mentalities, the classical and the historical, are present and operative in theology. But they cannot be easily recognized. Mentalities are not seen; only their conceptual articulations are heard. Deceptive situations can and do arise.

Old-fashioned and rigid classical mentality may masquerade among the faithful in newly-cut clothing. Or, genuine historical mentality may be present behind old-fashioned conservative thinking. A couple of simple examples show this better than a long explanation.

We all know the Catholic liberal who is intolerant and bitter towards his own Church, the Pope, and the conservative faithful. Yet, he shows compassion and understanding toward other Christian communities and their leaders. Possibly, before Vatican Council II, the same person had few good words, and even less charity, for Protestants. Then, he was a rigid defender of the Catholic faith; now, he is a champion of reform. Such an individual never went through a process of conversion. He simply exchanged one set of rigid concepts for another. He is as inflexible today as he ever was. He merely furnished his narrow mind with other ideas. True progress for him would have consisted in a movement toward more universal charity that embraces them all: Catholics, Protestants, Jews—all of God's children.

On the other side, we all know those faithful who are struggling to move along with changes. They are slowly coming to the appreciation of the new liturgy. They begin to see good in other religions. Yet, their pace is slow, halting and hesitating. They never have heard of historical mentality, but they have entered into the internal dynamics of change. They are far behind some pioneers, therefore they appear conservative. But, they are moving: they are part of the Church in evolution.

Philosophical Origins of the Two Mentalities

The discussion of the two mentalities inevitably raises the question about their origins.

The two widely differing mentalities arise from diverging philosophies of the process of knowing, sometimes explicitly held, sometimes assimilated existentially.

We should not think for one moment that esoteric speculations in the field of cognitional theory and epistemology influence only the professional philosophers. They are the ones who raise questions, advance hypotheses and advocate firm conclusions, but their answers filter down to ordinary people. Eventually, whole generations begin to live and act on the conclusions of philosophers.

The Greek crowd that assembled in the marketplace of Athens to listen to the Jew from Tarsus called "Paul," on the resurrection of the dead, murmured skeptically at the end of the discourse: "We shall hear you again." It is not likely that everyone in the audience was a philosopher, yet most probably each was deeply influenced by the dualistic explication of the nature of man that was so much in the air. Greek philosophers could not conceive of an immortal body; the body, by definition, was mortal. Hence, people in the marketplace rejected the doctrine of the resurrection.

Or, let us take a more recent example. Many of the defendants at the trial of war criminals at Nuremberg asserted that they were innocent since they acted on "superior orders," out of an innate sense of duty. They may not have known it, but, in all probability, they had been influenced by Kantian philosophy, which placed the moral imperative and sense of duty outside of the field of rational intellect.

Be that as it may in the case of the citizens of Athens or the defendants of Nuremberg, it seems to us undeniable that generations of Christians, through their education at all levels, through the catechesis and preaching they heard at all times, have unconsciously absorbed the basic principles of the classical mentality. They have thought of their faith, and ordered their lives, according to its principles. They have thought and acted according to a fairly well-defined cognitional theory.

At the root of the classical mentality there is a philosophical attitude, that of uncritical realism. Let us say more about it.

To say it without technical adornment, uncritical realism assumes that there is an essence in all things and this essence is appropriated through a universal concept by the human mind, bringing about an identity between the thing known and the person who knows it. Once the essence of a thing is in the mind, there is little room for expansion. Only accidents can be added, and they do not matter much. If those essences concern the truth of faith, a statement has an ultimate quality about it. Once the truth is known, we cannot go much beyond it. Once the essence of good order is known, we are not likely to improve on it. Change is likely to lead to disorder.

At the root of the historical mentality there is another philosophical assumption, that of critical realism.

Critical realism is rooted in the knowledge of external things, but it assumes that the information that reaches us is no more than raw material that has to be ordered and understood by the mind. This understanding is proportionate to the information available, but it does not come from there. It is generated by the mind, in the form of mysterious insights into the data received. Parallel with the ongoing process of information there is an ongoing process of producing insights. Man is not absorbing concepts or essences, only data; he himself generates insights into them, he gives them meanings. Such meanings are not capricious; they do not spring from some nebulous material; they bring precise understanding into the well-determined mass of information. As a precise meaning is finally confirmed as corresponding to the real, our knowledge progresses, a process that knows no end; and yet, at every stage it is linked to objective sources and resources, and measured by the exigence of truth. Man builds for himself, and lives in, a world of meanings.

This process should be sharply distinguished from any form of idealism that claims that we know nothing, or little, beyond the pre-set categories of our mind. We reject that.[4]

Penance

The great classical systems of theology that developed in the Middle Ages included, obviously, a scientific understanding of both the sacrament of penance and the moral principles of Christian life. Both were perceived ac-

[4]Joseph Maréchal, in his *critique* of the Kantian system, perceived an element, even within that system itself, on which the quest for the real can be built. It is the dynamic nature of the human mind, *le dynamisme de l'intelligence.* Man's relentless quest for more knowledge shows his insatiable desire for the infinite, since no finite object can or will ever satisfy his ongoing quest. The dynamic nature of the mind, which Kant himself describes, argues and proves the existence of an Absolute Being.

In other terms—dare we say it?—if Kant had been more alert in observing this dynamism of intelligence, and had drawn the logical conclusions, he would have been a transcendental Thomist!!

cording to the method of the classical mind. Their theology was articulated with the help of Aristotle's philosophy.

The sacrament of penance took its place among the seven great and efficacious signs of our salvation. Its essence was seen as composed of form and matter. After much dispute and hesitation, both elements became determined with some firmness. Absolution by the priest was the form; the confession of sins or the expression of sorrow by the penitent was the matter. For the first time in history, a firm theory was put behind the practices that arose in an existential way. The theory gave consistency to the understanding of the sacrament but brought with it rigidity as the "essence" of the sacrament became defined.

The new systematic vision was the end-product of a long evolution that began with creative practices and reached its peak with the definition of the essence of the sacrament. It brought new knowledge, but it also created obstacles for further development. No one could touch the substance of penance as defined. There was room only for accidental improvement in the giving and receiving of the sacrament.

When this happens, there is only one way of moving from classical understanding to historical perception: we must leave behind essential definitions and discover again the historically permanent elements in the sacrament.[5] Such elements can be found in the living practice of Christian communities, as the sacrament developed around the

---

[5]There is no healthier way of preserving authentic traditions than to search for the historically permanent elements in a mystery. The search will extend to the Scriptures, to the writings of the Fathers, to the pronouncements of the councils (which never wanted to canonize any philosophical school), to the devotional life of the faithful—that is to all the sources that are historical witnesses of living Christian faith.

To move from classical understanding to historical perception is to move closer to our traditions.

Mediterranean in the early centuries, as it evolved later in Ireland and other lands where Irish missionaries operated, or as it exists now in our Christian churches all over the face of the earth. Thus, we can find, as much as possible, the enduring core of our Christian tradition, as distinct from its particular historical expressions and accretions. We shall try to determine this in our fifth chapter, where we attempt to lay the foundations on which future practices can be built.

Systematic Moral Theology

The great scholastic theologians incorporated moral theology into their universal vision in a magnificent way. For them, there was no sharp dividing line between dogma and moral. It was an eminently sound approach. Unfortunately, it was not used by theologians in succeeding centuries, especially after the Council of Trent. We are still suffering from the split between dogmatic and moral theology, even if a more integrated vision is already emerging.

But, the limitations of the classical mentality affected moral theology too. There was a shift from the existential and concrete morality to an essential and abstract formulation of doctrine. The evangelical questions about persons, such as "who is a God-fearing man?" or "who is a person of evil heart?" were relegated to second place. The philosophical questions about the moral quality of acts, such as "what is intrinsically right?" or "what is intrinsically wrong?" took the first place.[6] Thus, a tightly-knit

[6]This was a search for the "essence" of the moral act—another expression of the classical mentality.

system of norms was developed, construed mainly with the help of metaphysical principles. In its early stages, strong cohesion with dogma kept a check on the enterprise. But once the separation between these two branches of theology became an accomplished fact, the development of moral theology was dominated more by human speculations than by critical reliance on sources of revelation. Acts were examined minutely; their moral quality defined exactly. Through the practical training of confessors, human opinions became absolute norms imposed on all who wanted to find peace with God.

In moral theology, too, there is a need to turn from the classical to the historical approach. We must return to our authentic sources, to Christian beliefs concerning morality. There we shall find the guidelines for Christians as they were taught by the Lord, as they were understood authentically by the Church. From the secure position of definitions by essences, we must move to the humble process of increasing our understanding, as much as we can, through the data and information that are available to us. The result may well be that, at times, we cannot speak with certainty, but must profess our ignorance by saying, "We do not know." A very Christian position! The Lord did not give us a vision of the full truth; he gave us his Spirit to lead us towards it slowly, painstakingly—historically.

We are changing beings, indeed. By understanding ourselves better, we understand the whole world differently. Once we know that we have no capacity to appropriate the essences of things around us, it becomes clear that we must revise the content of our knowledge. We lose some certainties in the process, but the new knowledge, limited as it is, brings us closer to reality. We develop by knowing ourselves better. Thus, we come to a better knowledge of God's presence and mighty deeds in our history.

(3) THE EXPANSION OF OUR FIELD OF VISION; OR, THE PROGRESS TOWARD BROADER HORIZONS

Every person sees as far as his horizon allows. It may be limited to the immediate neighborhood, or it may reach out far and wide to include fields and objects that are at a great distance. A person can expand his capacity to see, and move into new horizons.

A person changes as his capacity to see further increases. We say that his field of vision expands, or that he moves into broader horizons.

When someone climbs a mountain, the higher he is, the more he sees. As he climbs, his capacity to see increases. As his eyes embrace more and more, every object that he has known must be relocated within the new frontiers.

The village, that down in the valley appeared to him as the center of the earth, now is just one of the many places that dot the region. The river, that underneath gives life to men and beasts, appears from the height as a small brook that feeds into a mighty water course. When someone's field of vision expands, all things become different—because he has undergone a change, his capacity to see has been increased.[7]

---

[7]Franz Mussner, in his book *The Resurrection of Jesus,* explains well how development in understanding means development of the person himself:

   Who speaks of "hermeneutic" speaks of "understanding." The tireless efforts of Schleiermacher, Hegel and Dilthey concerning

From the example of the climber we could go to the experience of someone who flies over a whole region, or continent, or the surface of the earth, in a plane. Not only does he perceive many more things, he himself changes in the process. His capacity to know, to understand, to judge, develops through his experience.

What is true of physical ascent, and of the physical broadening of the field of vision, is true, analogously, of intellectual ascent. It is true when man is in search of understanding of God's mysteries.[8]

the hermeneutical question led to acknowledgment that the fundamental problem of hermeneutic is the relationship of the one who understands to the object of his understanding . . . To the information that enters into the process of understanding, the experiences of the person are added, experiences which can change the state of understanding subtly or quite radically. *Understanding changes—from the inside!* An old man understands the world differently from a young one who is inexperienced. An experience can be so intense, it can have such a strong impact on consciousness (existence) that the former understanding is totally overturned, and a wholly new understanding emerges and becomes possible. Understanding can grow and ripen organically; but, it can develop, also, through leaps and bounds (through some encounters, catastrophes, crises, singular life experiences, etc.) Someone may well say, *"Now* I understand, for the first time, the meaning of the world" (Franz Mussner, *Die Auferstehung Jesu,* pp. 140-141).

[8]Mussner describes forcefully how the experience of meeting the risen Christ changed the disciples:

The meeting with the risen Christ brought to the witnesses of the apparitions an *experience* as well, an experience that included *a new understanding* manifested in a new language. The "newness" of this understanding and language cannot be expressed through a clear formula; it is rooted in the Easter event itself. As the meaning of the Easter event cannot be rationally grounded, neither can the new understanding and new language be so explained. The risen one himself gives, through his apparitions, a new understanding and language; the new understanding and language, the new "way of seeing and speaking' ' has its origin and foundation in the risen one himself. The risen one becomes, for the witnesses of his apparitions, *the understood one,* because he gives himself to them as the one to be understood (Cf. Lk 24:31a "their eyes were opened and they recognized him"). The

Penance

The horizon of the Christian community has shifted many times in its history, and the shifts have affected the sacrament of penance. We can only point to some of those movements; we do not intend to describe them here. The Mediterranean churches of the early centuries did not cultivate the science of the theology of the sacraments. Their field of vision extended mainly to the need of the community to be holy in the eyes of God; they were the people of the new covenant, waiting for the coming of the Lord. Consequently, they saw sin in a strong social context, and they saw reparation for it as an act of expiation in the midst of the community. Even if an individual broke the covenant, the community had to remain firm in its commitment. If the offense was not condoned, the community remained holy.

The Irish churches saw sin and forgiveness within the horizon of the relationship between God and his erring child, perhaps on the pattern of the parable of the forgiving father, better known as the parable of the prodigal son. The instrument of reconciliation was the priest; the larger community played no part in it. They had a less acute awareness of the social dimension of sin.

A new expansion of horizons came with the scientific and systematic approach to the data of revelation in the Middle Ages. It emerged principally through the rediscovery of the philosophy of Aristotle. Theologians

risen one who reveals himself in the apparitions, "opens the eyes" of the witnesses and—behold!—they are seers, therefore understanders and proclaimers! A hermeneutical event! The Easter event inaugurates a hermeneutical process (*Ibid.*, p. 141).

were not satisfied any more with mere practical and existential solutions. They asked what were the essential components of the sacrament of penance. They sought to discover laws that were valid for all times. Once in possession of the knowledge of such laws, they thought they could regulate the life of the Church in general, and the granting of God's forgiveness in particular, for all time to come.

The horizon of the community changed many times. It moved from practice to theory, from existential attitudes to scientific knowledge.

Similar transformations took place in the understanding of sin.

Moral Theology

The Church did not begin by seeking a precise definition about the nature of sin and its various degrees. The local churches around the Mediterranean simply composed a list for the practical purpose of determining for what offenses penance should be granted. Those lists singled out some actions as significantly wrong, harmful "unto death"; but, they contained, also, sins that allowed degrees in culpability, such as "hurting one's neighbor," "being revengeful," "being greedy," and so forth. Not all wrong done to another warranted a long penitential life. Behind the hazy expressions there was the living person of the bishop who had to decide.

The picture was in some ways different, in some ways identical, in the Celtic communities in those far away islands northwest of the European shores. The pattern of the signs of forgiveness was different, but the mentality was similar. The Irish monks did not work out a theory. They did not operate on a scientific understanding of the word of God when they admitted the penitent to confession and assessed the necessary satisfaction. Nor did they go into long disquisitions about the various kinds of sins, such as happened later when theologians discussed the moral quality of divers human acts. All that the monks did was to balance the gravity of sin, as they understood it, with the weight of penance. Since forgiveness was given for any sin, there was no need to draw up lists of offenses for which penance would be granted. Every single sin, small or great, was good enough material for repentance. The priest's main problem was how to determine the fitting satisfaction. Hence, the origin of the penitential books. For all practical and existential purposes, such a procedure was sufficient.

The great scholastic theologians reached out far and wide in their effort to make theology into a science. They sought to find permanent laws behind changing practices. Their horizon expanded to the world of theory that should be the foundation for all practices. Their questions were about the abstract quality of good and evil that could be assigned to every act. Due to their teaching, the horizon of the community expanded too, from practice to theory, from the business of practical living to the scientific formulation of Christian ethics. A revolutionary change—even if people were not conscious of its happening.

Yet, the new achievement, which led to a real explosion of knowledge, was not without its own shortcomings.

Scholastic theologians did not have a thorough understanding of evolution, be it of the outside world known empirically, be it of the spirit of man known reflectively. Following their master, Aristotle, they handled metaphysical principles brilliantly, but they went too far in using them. They solved all sorts of physical, biological and psychological problems through metaphysics, when the facts would have warranted empirical observations and solutions according to the laws of physics, biology or psychology.

An example of such a shortcoming is the way they treated the issue of personal responsibility in a child. They assumed that responsibility required rationality, the capacity to know right from wrong. In that they were right. However, according to their metaphysical theories they had to assume that the essence of rationality was given all in one instant, since essences are one and indivisible. Because around the age of seven a child is usually able to read and write, they concluded that he must be given rationality around that time. Before it, the child could not form an intelligent judgment and could not make a responsible choice. After the blessed moment of receiving reason, or of reason emerging in him, he could decide his fate for heaven or hell; he was fully responsible. St. Thomas Aquinas, following such principles, says logically enough, but for us unconvincingly, that the moment a child comes to the use of reason he is fully able to decide between good and evil. Hence, his first act of reason will be either an act of love for God, or a revolt against him. He will be saved or damned accordingly.[9]

---

[9]Aquinas writes, in *Summa Theologiae* 1-2, q. 89, a.6:
    Whether venial sin can exist in a person with original sin alone.
    Reply: It is impossible that a person be guilty of venial sin along with original sin but not of mortal sin.

The new horizon of empirical sciences, in addition to that of metaphysics, was necessary to lead the community out of the rigid stance that it was compelled to take on the basis of a philosophical approach.

(4) MAN CAN MOVE FROM ONE STANDPOINT TO ANOTHER; AS HE DOES SO HIS PERCEPTION OF REALITY CHANGES

The specific standpoint of a person determines his angle of vision and his particular perception. He can mistakenly think that he sees everything around when, in fact, he sees only a segment of the universe. He must be dislodged from his position to have a more comprehensive perception of reality.

Change takes place in a human person when he moves from one standpoint to another. His field of vision becomes different. This is widely confirmed by our everyday experience, be it in a material, be it in a more spiritual, sense. If we take a walk in the country, the scenery we see

---

The reason: Before someone reaches the age of discretion, a lack of maturity impeding his use of reason excuses him from mortal sin, and so all the more from venial sin, should he do anything that is such objectively. When, however, a person has begun to have the use of reason, he is not entirely excused from the blame of venial and mortal sin. Now, at that point in life, the first thing a person is faced with is deliberation about his own self. Should he order his life in the direction of a rightful end, through grace, he will receive pardon for original sin. On the other hand, if he fails to direct his life to a true end, according to the measure of his capacity for discernment at such an age, he will sin mortally, failing, namely, "to do what in him lies" ' . . . (Translation by T.C. O'Brien. In *St. Thomas Aquinas: Summa Theologiae,* Latin text and English translation. London: Blackfriars, 1974, p. 95). See also *De veritate,* q. 28, a.3.

is determined by the spot where we have arrived. In a discussion concerning, let us say, human rights, the rights and wrongs we see around follow our previous philosophical stance on what man and human society are or should be. A believer in personal freedom will see things very differently from a follower of Marx. The analysis of this particular limitation in our perception is not so easy. To speak about a particular angle of vision is not much different from speaking about one's horizon. Granted that the two situations are close, that they may overlap, there is enough difference between them to prompt us to say that a specific type of change takes place when someone moves from one standpoint to another. Such a move is not quite identical with the expansion of horizon. It is, perhaps, best understood in the terms of dialectical movements.

In any human society there is a great deal of dialectical development, often more easily recognizable to historians than to those who live through it.

Progress is ordinarily initiated by new questions that sound disturbing to many people. It is continued through answers that prove satisfactory, and bring peace, to the community.

Such questions are often disguised in the form of practical action: a group of people begins to move, to act differently from all the rest. Others react and give strong emphasis to the values they feel are threatened. Thus, through questions and answers, through actions and reactions, through living forces that work dialectically, the social body moves ahead.

In such a situation only very few people are able to think with cool detachment and see the whole field of reality. The vast majority focus on what they perceive to be the right value and stress it, quite out of proportion to everything else.

Such living dialectics have been taking place in the Church ever since it was founded. They were present in the apostolic Church as we know from the *Acts of the Apostles* and the letters of Paul. Paul knew that justification did not come from the Law, but Christians coming from Judaism perceived a danger in his disregard for the Law. In their effort to save the traditions, they went far to discredit Paul. They even denied his right to call himself an apostle. Paul defended himself and his gospel passionately, and explained his doctrine of justification through faith forcefully, and one-sidedly, in the epistles to the Romans and the Galatians. Neither of those two letters is a detached and cool analysis of a problem such as can be found in the treatises of Thomas Aquinas. The adversaries of Paul had taken a specific standpoint for the support of the Law and judged his whole message accordingly. Paul reacted against their stance and explained his gospel from the opposite point of view.

The tragic confrontation among Christians in the sixteenth century was carried on dialectically—from standpoints that were diametrically opposed to each other. Many resented an excessive legalism and formalism in the Church. Relying on Paul, they reaffirmed that justice and sanctity come through faith alone. The bishops of the Council of Trent reacted strongly and stressed the need for laws and structures; they affirmed the value of good works and the efficacy of sacred signs and symbols, especially in the case of the seven sacraments.

After the Council, the "controversialists" on both sides carried on with the dispute. But they never got very far in solving the problems, still less in achieving reunion. Their dialectical standpoints were too far from each other. The tragedy is that what started as a dialectical exchange brought about rigid stances and perpetuated a rupture in the community. The unity of the Western Church was lost.

Modern ecumenical dialogues show, too, that the difference cannot be resolved through arguments. There is a need for both sides to retrace their steps, enlarge their field of vision so that it embraces a greater segment of reality, and then speak to each other again. Thus, the two sides can get closer to each other.[10]

Indeed, the internal development of the Catholic Church today cannot be understood unless we are aware that we are right in the middle of dialectical exchanges. Let us give just one example. The *Constitution on the Church in the Modern World* sees man and human society with an optimism that may well be encouraging but does not account for the evils of our century. It refers to the Scripture to demonstrate the goodness of this creation, but it does not tell us much about sin and its consequences present in our universe. The bishops expressed their profound faith in the value of the created world, but they said little about the evil that can penetrate it so deeply. In other terms, they told the truth but they felt no need to reaffirm the whole truth. Obviously, they were reacting against a widespread

---

[10]The method of pursuing theological reflections mainly through questions is far superior to the method of defending theses. Questions have the capacity to prompt a movement toward opening the mind to new discoveries and new understandings. Theses tend to close off any movement; they can even immobilize a person who is mindful only of defending his position.

It would be interesting to write a history of theological movements through questions asked in different ages. Most histories are written from the point of view of answers!

attitude that despised "the world"—that God loved so much that he gave his only begotten Son for it. They wanted to show that it is wrong to stress the importance of the other world to the point that the temporal welfare of our fellow-men becomes neglected. At the time of the Council, they did not feel the need to speak of the "world" that crucified the Lord of glory—and is still quite ready to do the same to the poor, weak and humble.

Once the historical standpoint of the bishops is known it is easy to fit the Constitution into the whole stream of development of ideas in Christian tradition. If it is not known, the result can be a distortion of Christian beliefs.[11]

Penance

The sacrament of penance obviously went through such dialectical developments. The Council of Trent, again, offers a good example. The reformers disclaimed any right in any man, whether priest or not, to judge the conscience of another, or to forgive sins in God's name. The Council reacted by affirming that the priest had the power to judge the penitent's disposition and to absolve him from his sins. The Fathers never intended to say that the priest should be like a judge-inquisitor. They rather meant that the priest is in possession of the highest judicial privilege, which is to show mercy and to grant free pardon to the offender, pro-

[11]No council in Christian history represents the whole truth. Every one of them must be inserted into, and interpreted in the context of, the whole ongoing tradition.

It is understandable that in the last decade much emphasis was given to the pronouncements of Vatican Council II, but, ultimately, what this last Council did or said cannot be understood without knowing what happened, and what was believed, before.

vided he is repentant.

But, subsequently, how many times was the Tridentine statement about the role of the priest as a judge misunderstood, and the sacrament transformed into a session of inquisitory inquiry! The standpoint of the Fathers of Trent makes good sense when its dialectical context is known. It leads to a new error if it is taken as an absolute statement of the full truth.

Moral Theology

Dialectics were not absent in the development of moral theology either. Since our purpose is not to narrate its history but to reach out for an illustration, we take just one point.

In the last centuries, the attention of theologians focused mostly on the individual, his acts and their consequences, eternal salvation or damnation. They had little perception of the social aspects of Christian morality. The cool reception of the papal encyclicals such as *Rerum Novarum, Quadragesimo Anno,* even of *Mater et Magistra*, testifies to that. Today, the opposite seems true: there is much talk about social sins and an over-indulgence concerning personal sins. To restore the balance, we should stress the duties imposed by justice, but we should give equal emphasis to the obligation to offer personal praise and reverence to God.

The examples could be multiplied, but we trust we have conveyed to the reader that, in so many ways, the knowledge and judgment of a person indeed depends on his particular standpoint in a universe that evolves with the help of dialectics. The Church, and we all in it, are part of this universe—and subject to its laws.

(5) PROGRESS IN UNDERSTANDING THROUGH INCREASINGLY COMPLEX CATEGORIES

Every human person trying to understand the world around him, and in him, operates with some categories of perception. They help him to bring order, cohesion and harmony into the disparate data perceived by his senses. But categories are human creations; they can be crude and simple, or sophisticated and complex. A person changes through the development of his mental categories.

Man develops, as he progresses in the use of increasingly complex mental categories, toward a better understanding of himself, of the world around him, of the transcendental realities Such change takes place not in persons only, but in communities as well.

Independently from any divine revelation, man always had some explanation of the universe in which he lived. For example, long before the theological concept of creation was elaborated, man came to an understanding of heaven and earth, and to an explanation of such natural phenomena as the shining sun or the falling rain. The earth was conceived of as a flat platform, possibly floating on an immense sea. There were waters above, too, separated from those below by the firmament, the sky. The sun traveled in the firmament; thus, there were day and night. God was the one who shaped the world, divided the waters and put the sun there. His actions were explained in primitive human categories. He was not unlike the potter of the ancient world who made all sorts of things, even small figurines, from the clay of the earth. So did God. Thus, the belief in a powerful being who gave life to man was expressed through the image of the potter forming the figure of man out of clay. God's mighty deeds were spoken of in categories known to man.

In a more subtle way, but no less really, a similar process has taken place throughout our Christian centuries. Every generation has had to use the conceptual and linguistic tools at its disposal to express its understanding of a transcendental God and to describe his interventions in our history.

As we mentioned earlier, in the scholastic understanding of the Middle Ages, each sacrament was conceived of as having its specific essence composed of matter and form. In the case of penance, the confession of sins, or the expression of contrition or attrition, was the matter; absolution, the form. There was an unerring Christian intuition behind those technical terms, a belief that God grants forgiveness to the contrite of heart through the ministry of the Church. The subtle distinctions between matter and form, even more between attrition and contrition, may not mean much to the modern mind not educated in scholastic categories, yet the fundamental intuition of those theologians was right, and of perennial validity. They expressed it in the scientific categories that were available to them.

Someone may well ask why it is necessary to employ a technical language or to use philosophical categories at all when we **want** to reflect on such ordinary simple Christian reality as the power to heal the broken-hearted. The answer is that it is hardly necessary, if we want to proclaim the mystery in its stark simplicity. But, if we want to understand something of the mystery, we need categories that embrace, and make intelligible, all sorts of things, human and divine. Medieval theologians had a conceptual system to understand the created universe. Through the same system, they tried to make the acts and deeds of God more intelligible. We do not behave in any different way, we just use other, and hopefully better, systems of thought. Man is naturally curious; he will never be content with the stark simplicity of a mystery.

Penance

The goodness and sinfulness of man is a mystery, too. As always, to understand it we must abide by the limitations of our categories—as they have developed through the centuries.

The early Church focused on the mystery, and dealt with the issue of sinfulness in a pragmatic way: sinners had to satisfy for their sins in the midst of the community, until they were judged—by the bishop—worthy to be readmitted into full communion. The Irish took a different approach, not less practical. Those who sinned had to do penance according to the judgment of the priest. In either case, sin was considered an awful mystery, but there was not much philosophizing about it.

Scientific categories were worked out for the state of grace, and for the state of sin as well, by medieval scholastic theologians. To be in the state of grace meant to be in God's favor, to have the capacity to participate in

God's life as his adopted child. To be in the state of sin meant the opposite, to be out of favor with God, serving the Evil One and carrying eternal death in one's own being. Venial sin, for the scholastics, was not sin in the same sense. There was no loss of eternal life in it: it was a refusal to grow in grace and wisdom.

The dividing line was drawn between the two types of sin in such a way that many actions, for which in the early Church no public penance was done, now fell on the side of mortal sin. For various reasons, the term "mortal sin" was applied to moral acts without the benefit of critical exegesis of the Scriptures, of the practical and doctrinal traditions of the Church. Hence, by the late Middle Ages, even more at the time of the Council of Trent, the number of mortal sins expanded considerably. Wrongful acts that in the early Church did not necessarily require public penance were included; so were acts by persons who, as a rule, were not allowed to enter the order of penitents, such as *iuvenes,* the young ones. In a practical way, hell became a greater menace for the Christian community than it ever was in the gospel and in the belief of the early communities. Damnation became a close threat hanging over the people for many more actions than before, and over people who earlier had been treated with more compassion, such as children.

Theologians could not conceive of a category of sin that would have comprehended serious evil, yet not to the point of a final break with God. The situation in moral theology, especially after Trent, could be compared to the state of medicine that would know of only two kinds of illness: terminal diseases and light indispositions, nothing between the two. The state of a person, to be intelligible, had to be clearly stabilized either in God's grace or in the power of the Evil One. So, while theologians wrote a great deal about the moral quality of human acts considered abstractly, they paid little attention to the internal dynamics that determined concretely the direction of life of a person.

Today we realize that there is such a thing as a seriously wrong action, without it being necessarily a sin unto death. Even ordinary experience teaches us that man is able to do wrong, and quite serious wrong, without revolting against God, without letting evil enter his heart as fully as Judas let darkness enter into his. We know, also, that relatively innocuous actions can be the sign of an internal movement toward death. Did not Judas betray the Lord with a kiss?

Let us acknowledge that, in this process of evolution, there are times when we have more questions than we can answer. Often enough, we must live with uncertainties. To progress in knowledge, we need increasingly sophisticated categories through which the mystery of the sacrament of penance, the relationship of man to God, can be better explained.

4

Fourth Question about the New Rite of Penance: What Is Its Meaning in an Evolutionary Process?

We are now ready and prepared to reflect on the *New Rite of Penance, Ordo paenitentiae,* that was promulgated in 1973. We ask: to what point of the evolutionary process does it take us?

To find the answer, ideally we would like to stand on a hilltop from where the development of the sacrament of penance could be surveyed. From there, we could see a procession of Christian communities aware of the gracious mercy of the Lord, trying to deal with the harsh reality of sin in their midst. From there, we could see the signs of one faith and of different procedures through which mercy was granted to the sinner, since

> the Church has faithfully celebrated the sacrament throughout the centuries—in varying ways, but retaining its essential elements ("Decree" of promulgation).

Such a scene would never be without some movement, without some development.

Indeed, on this scene appeared the new document, which is far more than a piece of paper or a set of rules. It is a humble instrument of God's mercy, in the sense that it tells the Church, with power, how to operate. Thus, it plays a role in the revelation of God's mercy to sinful man.

But, there should be no mistake about it, the document is not placed on the scene as a fixed monument—to stand there forever. It is part of an ongoing movement, of a never-ending process toward the discovery of full truth.

The *New Rite of Penance* is a living act of the Church. It feeds on nearly two thousand years of tradition and experience; it strikes new paths for the future. Therefore, as we try to evaluate its content and try to find out to what point of development it brings us, we must go well beyond its text. Our aim is to determine its role in the evolution of the sacrament and of moral theology, or, more correctly, in the evolution of the Christian community.

We proceed by three steps, indicated by three questions.

First, and quite simply, we ought to know what the new rules and regulations are, so we ask what is there. The *what* extends further than the basic reading of the text; we want to understand the meaning of the new dispositions.

Second, and more complexly now, we want to determine the point of development that the ideas or doctrines contained in the text have reached. The reader will remember that we said that ideas are living beings, therefore it is right to ask what point of maturity they have reached in this document. How far do they express the permanent content of Christian tradition? How far are they conditioned by our age?

Third, and with some trepidation, we want to know about the changing mentalities behind the evolving ideas and developing doctrines. The last source of any change is in a living person who himself can move from settled situations to pioneering efforts, from a classical conception of the world to an understanding of the historical process. He can broaden his horizons, he can take different standpoints and work out increasingly sophisticated categories to explain his universe. Hence, we ask what kind of mentalities are represented in the document.

Thus, we search for some understanding, in faith, of the *New Rite of Penance.*[1]

---

[1] We intend to do this search according to the principle laid down in our second chapter concerning the issue of doctrinal development: whenever a document is promulgated with authority, and thus is a significant con-

(1) WHAT IS THE CONTENT OF
ORDO PAENITENTIAE?

Besides the formal decree of promulgation by the Sacred Congregation for Divine Worship, the document contains three parts, each with a distinct purpose. They are:

    (a) an introduction, *praenotanda,* of doctrinal character;

    (b) the description of three rites, *ordines,* with sample readings and prayers;

    (c) three *appendices* of sundry dispositions.

(a) The Introduction

The *praenotanda* are really more than what we ordinarily understand by "introduction." The beginning of it reads as a *profession of faith in the mystery of reconciliation in our salvation history.* As creeds do, it recapitulates God's saving deeds

> The Father has shown forth his mercy by reconciling the world to himself in Christ and by making peace for all things on earth and in heaven by the blood of Christ on the cross (*Ordo paenitentiae,* #1).

---

tribution to development, the weight of the document must be assessed. Respect must be given to authority, but precisely as far as it is demanded by the nature of the act; its importance should not be either downgraded or upgraded.

    Our purpose is, therefore, to come to a detached theological judgment. Our aim is not pastoral. Theological judgment gives a critical evaluation of the content. Pastoral writings aim to facilitate the implementation of the new rite. Both approaches are legitimate, but they should be clearly distinguished from each other. They are works of different literary forms.

Jesus announced the kingdom and granted forgiveness to those who repented. Through his death and resurrection, he instituted the new covenant between God and man. But, his work has not come to an end; he has given power to the apostles to forgive sins. They proclaimed the good news all over the world, and the Church assumed the ministry of mercy through the mysteries of Baptism, the celebration of the Eucharist, and through explicitly granting forgiveness to those who sinned after their baptism (cf. #1-2).

There follows a short description of the *reconciliation of penitents in the life of the Church*. There is the paradox:

> the Church, which includes within itself sinners . . . is at the same time holy and always in need of purification (#3).

Through manifold penitential exercises, sins are forgiven, holiness is granted to God's people. Thus, the Church is a sign of man's conversion to God. There are many ways of imploring God's mercy but, among them, the sacrament of penance takes a prominent place. Through it the sinner obtains pardon from God, and is reconciled with the Church. All sins offend God, and harm the Church; the two effects cannot be separated. Therefore, the sinner must be reconciled with both his God and his Church (cf. #3-5).

The text turns to describe the sacrament of penance in its parts which are contrition, confession, satisfaction, and absolution. It does not raise the question of the relative importance of each, either historically or doctrinally. It distinguishes clearly, however, those situations in which the sacrament is necessary for salvation and those in which it is useful. This is the recapitulation of an old medieval distinction between *sacramenta necessitatis* and *sacramenta utilitatis.* In the case of a person who has gravely offended God, reconciliation is necessary. In the case of one who experiences his weakness every day, penance is useful (cf. #6-7):

> Just as the wound of sin is varied and multiple in the life of individuals and of the community, so too the healing which penance provides is varied. Those who by grave sin have withdrawn from the communion of love with God are called back in the sacrament of penance to the life they have lost. And those who through daily weakness fall into venial sins draw strength from a repeated celebration of penance to gain the full freedom of the children of God (#7).

There are *offices and ministries instituted for the reconciliation of penitents.* The document stresses the role of the community in the celebration of penance: the Church is the instrument of conversion and the source of pardon; however, it grants absolution through ordained ministers, bishops and presbyters:

> the Church becomes the instrument of the conversion and absolution of the penitent through the ministry entrusted by Christ to the apostles and their successors (#8).

Canon law regulates the exercise of their ministry of pardon: they need proper authority to exercise it. But to minister well, they must have higher gifts. They should be able to recognize God's work in the hearts of men; they should continue the ministry of Christ. Yet, the sacrament does not come from the priest alone; the repentant sinner plays his own part in it. He proclaims and celebrates God's mercy in union with the whole Church:

> Thus the faithful Christian, as he experiences and proclaims the mercy of God in his life, celebrates with the priest the liturgy by which the Church continually renews itself (#11; cf. also #8-11).

The text takes an increasingly practical turn: it gives norms for *the actual celebration of the sacrament of penance.* It can be administered in three different forms:

(a) the rite for the reconciliation of individual penitents;

(b) the rite for several penitents with individual confession and absolution;

(c) the rite for several penitents with general confession and absolution (cf. #12-35).

Since these dispositions overlap to a large extent with the main body of the document where the new rite is given in detail, we describe them separately below.

Penitential services can be of great help to lead the community to a deeper conversion of heart and to a renewal of life, through listening to the word of God together, meditating on it, and by prayers offered together. While their structures could be patterned on the rite of penance for the reconciliation of several penitents, they should not be confused with the sacrament. They are useful for all, young and old:

> Penitential celebrations, moreover, are very useful in places where no priest is available to give sacramental absolution. They offer help in reaching that perfect contrition which comes from charity and enables the

faithful to attain to God's grace through a desire for
the sacrament of penance (#37; cf. also #36-37)

The Introduction concludes by giving directions for *the
adaptation of the rites to various regions and circumstances.* Adaptation means reasonable application of
the norms, it does not mean changing them in any significant way. Detailed rules describe the competence of the
episcopal conference, of the bishop, of the priest, in this
process of adaptation to specific needs. In the case of
general absolution, however, the power of the bishop
seems to be broader than mere reasonable application: it is
left to him, with consultation with other members of the
episcopal conference, to determine that the conditions for
the granting of such absolution exist. More of this later (cf.
#38-40).

Thus, the Introduction, which is really an extensive
previous explanation for the proper celebration of the
rites, ends.

(b) Practical norms: the Rites

The second part of the document contains the three
rites, the *ordines,* the sacramental signs and symbols in a
broader sense.

The rite for the reconciliation of an individual penitent
encourages the priest and the penitent to respond to God's
mercy together. There is a personal exchange between the
two; their meeting is more than a casual and ritual performance. They mutually greet each other; then, they read
an appropriate passage from the Holy Scriptures. They
pray before the penitent confesses his sins. Then, the priest

gives advice, and imposes satisfaction. Finally, he invokes God the Father's mercy and, in his name, gives the penitent absolution. In doing so, the priest may impose his hands on the penitent or extend them toward him. Together they acknowledge, by prayer of praise, the gift of pardon, before the penitent is dismissed with words of peace and encouragement (cf. #15-20 and #41-47).

In the case of necessity, the document allows for a shortened version of the form. It consists of no more than the bare confession of sins, imposition of penance and absolution. The sacramental process is stripped to the essentials, as in fact it has been known to millions of the faithful in recent centuries (cf. #22 and #44).

The rite for the reconciliation of several penitents with individual confession and absolution is a combination of new and old. The preparation for the reception of the sacrament and the thanksgiving after it are done in community. All those present pray for God's mercy and acknowledge it, but the actual giving and receiving of the sacrament remains private and individual.

The preparation in community follows the model of the liturgy of the Word before the Eucharist. The congregation listens to readings from the Scriptures followed by a homily. They observe a period of silence for the examination of conscience, after which they recite a prayer of repentance such as the *Confiteor* or one of the penitential psalms. There the communal celebration ceases and individual confessions follow, with personal absolution granted by the priest. The celebration is concluded with a prayer of praise and thanksgiving in community (cf. #31-34 and #48-59).

The rite for the reconciliation of several penitents with

general confession and absolution follows the pattern described above, but there are no individual confessions. Absolution is given to all by the presiding priest. The norm for the use of this rite is in the expression *gravis necessitas requiritur:* it can be used in case of serious need.

Being in danger of death is an obvious example of such a grave need. The document gives another one: the penitents will not be able to receive the sacrament in its usual form for a long time to come.

Again, the celebration ends with praise and thanksgiving, but the priest is enjoined to warn the penitents that they must confess their sins individually whenever they can do so (cf. #35 and #60-66).

(c) The Appendices

In the Appendices, we find directions for absolution from censures, for dispensation from irregularities, and sample structures of penitential services for different seasons such as Lent or Advent, or for different people such as children, youngsters and the sick. There is also a model for the examination of conscience.

****

There is no doubt that the *New Rite of Penance* is a living act of the Church. It feeds on nearly two thousand years of tradition and experience; it strikes new paths for the future and represents an important development. Once we have ascertained what it contains, we must investigate further to discover the theological insights that inspired its norms and dispositions.

(2) WHAT ARE THE EVOLVING IDEAS IN
ORDO PAENITENTIAE?

Now we move to a deeper level. We look for the movement of ideas behind the external changes, that is we try to determine the development of doctrine that the changes represent. Our interest is broader than simply describing new ideas. We are interested in the old and the new, even more in the transition from one to the other. We are interested in a movement of life. And, given the close connection between the sacrament of penance and the understanding of sin, we are interested in the development of doctrine concerning both issues.

One issue is relatively easy to dispose of. There is no sign in the *Ordo paenitentiae* of an awareness of any development of doctrine that has taken place recently in moral theology and could affect the administration of the sacrament. On this, there is no word. Does the document simply presume the validity of the moral theology current before Vatican Council II? Or, does it try to avoid the question?

At any rate, its silence is a deficiency. After all, the Mediterranean churches determined the process of forgiveness according to their understanding of sin—and so did the Irish churches. Can we today renew the process of pardon without asking, again, what sin is?

Yet, those who drafted *Ordo paenitentiae* may have faced the issue and decided not to take any notice of post-conciliar developments. They may have thought that, because moral theology was in fermentation, there should be no changes in the process of forgiveness. If this is so, we must wait for better times when a fuller integration of the understanding of Christian morality and the sacrament of penance will be possible.

It is much more difficult to answer the question whether the *Ordo* represents a significant development in the understanding of the sacrament of penance.

Most certainly there are new developments in the three rites. They show healthy evolution in the field of liturgy, by expanding signs and symbols; and in pastoral theology, by allowing a more personal approach to the sacraments.

But, what about "development of dogma"? Does the document represent any progress? If so, is it significant?

The answer does not come readily.

The Introduction speaks in terms so general that, logically, several constructions are possible. It can be taken as the summary of much that is good in current theology, but as going no further. It can serve also as a starting point for theologians who are in search of new insights.[2]

The Introduction reads as a profession of faith in the sacrament of penance. It is very scriptural, heavily loaded with quotations. Our overall response can hardly be anything else than the traditional, "Amen, amen."[3]

[2]Since the publication of the *Ordo paenitentiae,* there have been ample comments on the Introduction. On the whole, we feel that more has been read into the text than is actually contained in it. It is a most valuable text in the sense of general statements about our faith. It contains many elements in the solid possession of the Church at the time of its publication. It pulls them all together, and thus it is valuable. It is innovative only when it is compared to doctrines contained in some preconciliar manuals of dogmatic theology, moral theology or canon law. But, those manuals had already been superseded by better publications in 1973, when the new *Ordo* was published.

[3]Indeed, the literary form of profession of faith would fit the Introduction best. Its intention is clearly to recapitulate the best elements in Christian doctrine, as they have been held throughout history, about the power and process of forgiveness in the Church. A piece of such literary form must always be handled carefully. Its purpose is precisely to remain on a general level and not to enter into details. Therefore, only very general conclusions can be drawn from it. It is not meant to decide disputes among theological schools.

But, let us see it more in detail. The *Constitution on the Church, Lumen Gentium,* had its impact on the Introduction. The Church is presented as God's own chosen people; somehow the whole community plays a part in reconciling sinners to God.

The social dimension of every sinful act, as of any good deed, is stressed:

> "By the hidden and loving mystery of God's design men are joined together in the bonds of supernatural solidarity, so much so that the sin of one harms the others just as the holiness of one benefits the others." Penance always entails reconciliation with our brothers and sisters who are always harmed by our sins (#5).

This may be new to those who do not know our traditions. It is certainly not new to anyone who has followed the evolution of doctrine about the mystical unity of the Church. For a long time, the corporate nature of grace has been known and stressed no less than the harm done to the whole body by the sin of one member.

The integral parts of the sacrament of penance are explained in terms that are general enough to avoid any controversy; they are contrition, confession, satisfaction and absolution.[4] Clearly, there would have been no point in

---

[4]Satisfaction as it is understood today has little in common with satisfaction as it was understood either in the early Mediterranean churches or in the Irish churches. Today it is a small devotional act or some small good deed that can hardly be said to be in proportion to the wrong committed. While, theoretically, many writers call it important to the point of being an integral part of the sacrament, when the practice is observed we have to admit that it has become so small and insignificant that it plays no major role in the sacrament. In reality, it is a small imposition to strengthen the resolve of the penitent and to make

reviving the subtle discussions about attrition and contrition. Nor is the text trying to determine what is of the essence of the sacrament. The disputed questions are not touched on; in effect, they are left open to be disputed.

The distinction between the reconciliation of those who have sinned gravely and the devotional reception of the sacrament by others is stated first in scriptural terms. There are those who need the sacrament to be restored to life:

> the Father receives the repentant son who comes back to him, Christ places the lost sheep on his shoulders and brings it back to the sheepfold, and the Holy Spirit sanctifies this temple of God again (#6).

There are those who take the sacrament to increase their own strength and their freedom to praise God:

> This is not a mere ritual repetition or psychological exercise, but a serious striving to perfect the grace of baptism so that, as we bear in our body the death of Jesus Christ, his life may be seen in us ever more clearly (#7).

The distinction is repeated in the terms of medieval canon law: for some, penance is a sacrament of necessity; for others, a sacrament useful for spiritual progress. Strangely enough, as one reads further, it seems that these two distinct operations of penance are lost from sight; the very term "reconciliation" is used indiscriminately for both, although in its proper sense it should be used for those who

him pray for God's grace. Yet, the weight of tradition is so heavy that most theologians would be reluctant to admit that satisfaction in the ancient sense has disappeared from the structure of the sacrament or that, if it has been retained, it plays only a nominal role.

"have left the house of their Father," not for those who have remained there.

The ministers of the sacrament are the bishop and the priest. The bishop supervises its administration. The priest needs faculties—although, obviously, he needs wisdom and prudence even more, and these can be given by the Holy Spirit alone.

Penitential services should be clearly differentiated from the sacrament of penance. They can do much good, but they are not the sacrament.

Under the heading of "Adaptations," the power of episcopal conferences of diocesan bishops, and the power of priests, is discussed. The right to adapt the norms to different places and circumstances is rather limited. It hardly amounts to more than what is known as "reasonable interpretation" in canon law.

There is one important provision, however. It is the right of the bishop to determine when the conditions for granting general absolution exist. They are mortal danger and "grave need." There is no problem in defining mortal danger: circumstances from which death may follow, even if its actual probability is remote. Grave need is more difficult to determine. The text gives one example:

> namely when, in view of the number of penitents, sufficient confessors are not available to hear individual confessions properly within a suitable period of time, so that the penitents would, through no fault of their own, have to go without sacramental grace or holy communion for a long time (#31).

An alert interpreter will immediately ask if the application of "grave need" must be restricted to the one case described, or if it can be extended to analogous situations. In other terms, is the case really the naming of the one possible grave need outside of which none can exist; or, is it an example out of many possible "need situations" which can emerge, with certain variety, in different places at different times?[5]

This is no mere quibble about language. The answer has far-reaching practical consequences.

There are good reasons to think that the case is given as an example or illustration, not as an exclusive enumeration.

First, it would not have made much sense to speak of mortal danger and grave need if the only need recognized is the absence of priests. It would have been more logical for the legislator to say simply that there are two cases, mortal danger and absence of priests; or, to say that there are two needs, mortal danger and absence of priests. The construction of the text seems to indicate that the absence of priests stands there as an *analogatum princeps,* a prime analogy, that admits similar cases.

Second, it is a sound principle of interpretation in canon law that whenever there is a favor granted, it must be interpreted broadly. Now, the power to absolve is, indeed, a favor. Therefore, its extent must be interpreted broadly, that is, its use can be extended to situations analogous to the one case given.

We are not discussing something in the abstract. The issue is the real power of the bishop. The document says:

---

[5]In the technical language of canon law, is the one case given *taxative* (as fixed enumeration, no more can be added) or *exemplificative* (as an example, more could be found)? *En quaestio!*

The judgment about the presence of the above conditions and the decision concerning the lawfulness of giving general sacramental absolution are reserved to the bishop of the diocese, who is to consult with the other members of the episcopal conference (#32).

But the extent of the bishop's power depends on the interpretation of the conditions. Is his power restricted to the mere recognition of the presence of mortal danger or absence of priests? Or, is his power extended to the recognition of "grave need situations" on the basis of the example given in the text? We think the second interpretation is legitimate.

Someone may well object that the text is too obscure to allow any interpretation to be proposed with certainty. In response, we willingly admit that there is some ambiguity in the text, but then the rule for the interpretation of ambiguous texts must come into play, and that rule is clear: in case of doubt, the broader meaning can be given to the text. It follows, therefore, that the bishop has the right to determine whether or not, in given circumstances, grave need exists and, consequently, general absolution can be granted. His prudent judgment is respected.

This is a significant provision for the future: grave need is not defined abstractly, it is left to the bishop to acknowledge its existence concretely. Local conditions can be taken into account.

If the Introduction is compared to some pre-Vatican II manuals on the sacrament of penance, there is no doubt that it shows some progress. But, if it is compared to the documents of Vatican II, there is little evidence of further development.

But, after all, there are the new "rites." If they do not

spring from a new doctrinal insight, where do they come from? We shall try to answer this question in the next section.

(3) WHAT ARE THE SIGNS OF EVOLVING MENTALITIES?

Our intention now is to reflect on the *Ordo paenitentiae* with the aim of discovering any sign that may indicate movement and development from one mentality to another. This is the last step in our inquiry: we cannot go any further, on the human level, in exploring the meaning of the document. Of course, beyond it all, there is another dimension—the inspiration of the Spirit—but that is not directly ascertainable to mortal theologians.

(a) The Settler and the Pioneer

The reader will remember the parable of the settler and the pioneer.

There are signs of the mentality of the pioneer in our document.

There are new liturgical structures. The granting of forgiveness is not reduced any more to bare essentials. There is a "celebration" where none existed before. In the reconciliation of individual persons, the priest and the penitent are nourished by the word of God; they are united in common prayer, together they ask for mercy and give thanks for it. The sacrament unfolds its internal riches; the signs and symbols are expanded to the benefit of the priest and the penitent. The pioneering mind is even more evident in the structure for reconciling several penitents; it is a community celebration. The group is united in listening to the word of God. It is knit together by the people's common awareness of their own sinfulness and of their need for God's mercy. The sacrament brings together, sustains and shapes the community.

The new rite creates new pastoral situations. The relationship between the priest and the penitent is not covered by obscure anonymity; ideally, they meet face to face. The opportunity is there for the penitent to review his life with the help of a presumably wise guide. The aim is not only to obtain absolution with the determination of some satisfaction, but also to find a new direction in life, a new strength in the service of the Lord.

Many of these liturgical and pastoral innovations spring from a renewed awareness that a Christian does not live or act alone, but as a member of the community. This social dimension is part of the new rite, less when reconciliation is granted individually, more when it is granted in a community celebration.

These are signs of "conversion"—of turning—from a monotonous rite to a living celebration, from impersonal administration to personal care. As so many good initiatives, they are not without some risk. It is a risk for a sinner to present himself in full daylight (metaphorically speaking) to a priest whom he does not know, and to open himself not only to the rite of forgiveness, but also to a certain amount of direction. After all, ordination does not necessarily confer the charism of discretion!

It is a risk for the Church to impose the demands of the new rites on the clergy, demands that are likely to prove themselves much heavier than it is assumed at present.

The new rites require a somewhat prolonged exchange

between the individual penitent and the minister of pardon. They also demand careful preparation for community celebrations. Such liturgies, to be meaningful, require time, and much time. The old pattern of parish life that allowed for confessions for a few hours over the weekend is too restrictive to satisfy the new order. If the clergy of a parish want to live up to their task, they should be ready to receive penitents throughout the week—mornings, afternoons and evenings. Moreover, they need theoretical knowledge and practical wisdom in greater measure than ever before. In individual confession, the penitent is in a delicate position; he is expected to open his whole being to God's minister, and to listen to him as he speaks with a cloak of authority that may give more weight to his advice than it deserves. The unwary can be easily misled by an incompetent or imprudent counselor. Candidates for ordination should be thoroughly trained in every branch of theology, pastoral counseling, and should pray intensely for wisdom, which is a rare commodity hardly ever given by God to those who are humanly not well-prepared. After ordination, the same process of study and prayer should continue.[6]

---

[6]For intelligent and helpful advice both wisdom and learning are necessary. When the penitent asks the priest for help in a case, often enough the question concerns Christian doctrine; the penitent wants enlightenment. When this happens, it is unfair to tell him simply "Follow your conscience, that is all." Of course. he should follow his conscience and nothing else, but if he is in need to know more about Christian tradition concerning our way of life, he is perfectly entitled to ask for advice. It is not for nothing that the community supported a priest for so many years in studies; he should know with some precision about the evangelical origins of a point of doctrine, and its subsequent development over the centuries. And, he should repay the community by imparting some knowledge to the penitent.

To say that each should follow his conscience is absolutely true. Ul-

The issue points even further: we are in sore need of renewing the office of parish priest, not in theory—we have plenty of beautiful texts—but in practice. Often enough, our parish clergy is occupied in managerial tasks, in supervising the construction of new buildings, in maintaining old ones, in raising funds, in being the heart and soul of various parish works and associations. They have little time left for prayer, reflection, reading, and for the personal care of the faithful.[7] The words of the Twelve come to mind, as they are quoted in the *Acts of the Apostles:*

Now in these days when the disciples were increasing in number, the Hellenists murmured against the Hebrews because their widows were neglected in the daily distribution. And the twelve summoned the body of the disciples and said, "It is not right that we should give up preaching the word of God to serve tables. Therefore, brethren, pick out from among

timately, we have nothing else to follow, and God himself will judge us on our fidelity to our conscience. But, in rational beings the conscience should operate intelligently. It should see what is right and wrong. It should know, through well-grounded reasoning or the light of faith, why something is right or wrong.

To sum it up, the priest is under obligation to share his learning with his fellow Christian who asks for advice. To tell him simply to follow his conscience and leave him in darkness is no help. It is like leaving someone in a dark forest at night, telling him to follow his instinct to find the way out!

But let us say this clearly, too. It is not the business of the priest to make the ultimate concrete judgment over an action. He should tell the penitent about the doctrine, the penitent should know his own circumstances, and then the final concrete judgment on a course of action should be made by the penitent himself. Thus, we have the right balance. The autonomy of the person is respected, and service is done to him by offering him information about our tradition whenever he needs it.

[7]There is a strange paradox there. A pastor may have to spend most of his time on tasks for which he has had no preparation, and he has little time left for tasks that he was prepared for in the seminary.

you seven men of good repute, full of the Spirit and of wisdom, whom we may appoint to this duty. But we will devote ourselves to prayer and to the ministry of the word." And what they said pleased the whole multitude, and they chose Stephen, a man full of faith and of the Holy Spirit, and Philip, and Prochorus, and Nicanor, and Timon, and Parmenas, and Nicolaus, a proselyte of Antioch. These they set before the apostles, and they prayed and laid their hands upon them (Acts 6:1-6).

But, how can the parish clergy devote themselves to prayer and to the ministry of the Word when other needs are pressing?

The answer may well come in giving a greater role to the permanent deacons. They could take over much of the work done by presbyters now. They could take care of buildings, old and new, they could look after the poor and the sick, so that their "elders" could devote themselves to prayer and to the ministry of the Word. The sacrament of penance is part of this ministry of the Word in more than one way: in his advice, the priest should speak the Word; in imparting absolution, he does proclaim God's word of mercy.

The *New Rite of Penance,* like leaven, may "ferment the mass" in our parishes beyond our expectation, if clergy and faithful alike live up to its demands.

There are, indeed, signs of a pioneering mentality in the new rite.

But, what about signs of the settler's mind? Let us be clear though. By settler, we do not mean a Christian who is faithful to his traditions; in that sense, we are all settlers. Rather, we mean the fellow in the gospel who received his talents and hid them in the ground for fear of losing them.

He succeeded in preserving them intact, but he had no profit either. Are there signs of such a mentality in our document?

Yes. The theology of the sacrament, on which the liturgical and pastoral innovations are built, is virtually identical with the theology of penance as it developed in the post-Tridentine centuries. There is hardly any new insight, any new understanding beyond that.

For instance, according to the post-Tridentine theology, the sacramental pardon must not be given to the faithful in any other way than through individual confession and absolution, except in the case of some extreme emergency. The *Ordo* upholds the same discipline, presumably on the same theoretical grounds. It requires individual reconciliation in all ordinary cases. Such a stance is likely to lead to practical situations fraught with contradictions.

For example, the rite for the reconciliation of individual penitents *(First Form)* encourages a prolonged exchange between the priest and the penitent. The rite for the reconciliation of several penitents with individual confession and absolution *(Second Form)* is bound to discourage any such thing. The reason is simple: the whole group must go to confession and receive absolution individually before they can give thanks for God's pardon in common. The result can hardly be anything else than short confessions followed by quick absolutions. The liturgical and pastoral situation, carefully built up in the first form, is virtually destroyed in the second.[8]

---

[8]Many priests who, since the introduction of the new rite, have taken part in the administration of the sacrament according to the second form can already report from experience on the unsatisfactory aspects of such celebration. The usual pattern is as follows:

There is no doctrinal reason why absolution could not be given in common to the members of a group who manifest their desire to receive it and who, although deeply aware of their sinfulness, are not conscious individually or collectively of a grave offense against God.[9]

On the eve of a feast, a penance service is announced; a large group of penitents gathers in the church. Priests are not available in large numbers. Before the ceremony starts, the priests are advised to refrain from giving advice as much as possible, and to be expeditious in granting absolution.

The service starts with the introductory rites in common. Then the available priests take up positions at various points of the church. It should be understood that private rooms for confession are not available in large numbers either. Hence, for the most part there is a meeting between the priest and the penitent in view of the whole congregation, obviously the least suitable situation for serious counseling. So confessions are heard passively, and absolution is given without delay.

Many objections that were raised against the old rites can be raised all over again, and more strongly so!

We do not insinuate that there are no better and more satisfactory patterns. We simply want to say that if there is a large number of penitents, and a small number of priests and places available, there is no way of administering the sacrament in its second form according to the lofty principles stated in the first form.

[9]This statement may be in need of explanation. The initial question is really not about a group but about a person: can anyone receive absolution who confesses his sinfulness in general terms but declares no sin in particular? Many classical textbooks claim that such procedure would not be enough since there is no proper matter for absolution. Therefore, they give the advice that the penitent should find some "small sins" or confess some sin from the past again; thus he provides matter for the sacrament. One could object immediately that the so-called "small sin" may or may not have been a sin before God. Moreover, if the past sin has been confessed and forgiven before, the penitent is confessing nothing; therefore, there would be no matter. But, indeed, there is no indication in Christian tradition that the matter must be necessarily an individual act reported by the penitent. Confession in general terms, such as is found in the *Confiteor,* should be enough.

If an individual person can receive absolution after confessing his sins in general terms, there is no reason whatsoever why a group of persons, declaring their sinfulness together and asking for healing, could not receive absolution in common.

Obviously, we are not speaking of those who are bound to seek reconciliation for "sins unto death."

Further, the insistence on individual confession and absolution in every single case is bound to militate against the frequent reception of the sacrament otherwise encouraged in the document. The intense spiritual encounter that the first rite recommends is likely to be beneficial only if it happens with judicious rarity. Strong nourishment too often is too much. Hence, the very observance of the new rite may work against receiving it frequently.

Perhaps the rigid theological stance on the individual reception of the sacrament springs from an uncritical acceptance of moral theology as it developed in the post-Tridentine centuries. If a fundamental break with God is an ordinary event in the Christian community, the ordinary practice should indeed be person-to-person reconciliation. If, on the other hand, such a break is as rare as the penitential discipline of the ancient Church presumed it, the ordinary practice may well be in common repentance and common absolution.

Let us be fair, however. It would be unreasonable to expect from the drafters of an official document on the discipline of penance, promulgated in these turbulent post-Vatican II years, that they would have based it on new but not fully proven insights. Fair enough. But then we should be aware that we are dealing with a document conceived precisely for these turbulent times.

(b) Classical and historical mentality

The *Ordo paenitentiae* displays, in several ways, a movement from the classical to the historical mentality.

The freer winds of liturgical renewal have penetrated into the penitential discipline and have brought healthy changes through the idea of celebrating God's mercy in expanded and adaptable rites. The winds of pastoral renewal, too, have made their impact. The new rites allow many possibilities for creative approaches, for adaptations suitable for different persons and groups. Through such a process, priests and faithful are invited not only to follow the rules but to create them, and thus to enter into a more historical existence.

But, the *Ordo* is very restrained when it touches on theological principles. It shuns legitimately disputed questions. It does not encourage reflection or initiatives to increase our theological understanding. It displays a rigid concept of the "essence" of the sacrament, especially when describing its parts analytically. They appear unchangeable (cf. #6).

(c) Horizons

Does the new *Ordo* expand our horizons?

The redactors of the document clearly realized the need for the renewal of the sacramental signs and symbols. In that their horizons extended beyond previous practices; so do ours, if we follow them. But, did the redactors see the immense problem, acute especially in many European countries, of the large number of Christians being present at the Eucharist and yet not sharing in it? Those churchgoers must be "graced people" because they believe in the Eucharist, yet apparently they are resisting grace since they do not take communion. Their situation looks even more bewildering when it continues from year to year, perhaps for a whole life, with an exceptional communion at Eastertide or Christmas. Are those Christians really dead members of the Church? Or, are they living members who, out of some mistaken conception of God's mercy, are not joining the Lord's table but just looking at it from a distance? Can such habitual and widespread alienation from the Eucharist be healed through penance?

Can it be that those persons are living members of the community but infirm, in sore need of being healed and strengthened? Can that be accomplished by the sacrament of penance? Can it be accomplished through pardon granted in common? If so, would they be better disposed afterwards to come for individual guidance and help; would they be willing, then, to receive the sacrament personally?

Such pastoral problems do not seem to be within the horizon of the *New Rite.*

Repentance was the primary condition of entry into God's kingdom preached by Jesus. In the same spirit, today, repentance is more important for the renewal of the Church than any reforming of the structures. Everyone in the Christian community is in some way wounded by sin and, therefore, in need of healing; everyone is weak and, therefore, in need of strengthening. It follows that all should have an easy access to the sacramental source of grace or, more precisely, to the healing and strengthening gesture of Christ through the ministry of the Church. But there is no good provision for such easy access. Although the *Ordo* encourages the frequent use of the sacrament, it offers no good practical way of doing it.

The full potential of the sacrament to help a community to progress in Christian life may not have been manifest to the redactors. There is such a thing as sin by a community, be it through commission or omission. It could consist in subtle prejudices, biased actions, never-articulated oppression of the weak. To bring a community together, make them aware of their common sinful attitudes and acts, lead them to repentance, and give the sacrament to them by common absolution, makes good sense. A penance service does not fulfill the same purpose. The more a community sins, the more it needs a powerful remedy.

(d) Dialectics

In these post-Vatican II years, the Church is going through a process of dialectical developments. Much of what is said and done today is conceived and enacted in reaction to the past. Our times are not those of quiet growth, but of actions and reactions, of theses and antitheses, of a pendulum swinging right and left. This may be disturbing, but it is a historical fact.

The overall defensive attitude of the Catholic Church, ever since the Reformation, caused too much tension to be built up. When the forces of life claimed their right again, not all changes came peacefully. By nature's laws, this was likely to happen. Good wine is the product of violent fermentation.

Dialectical attitudes can be discovered even in the conciliar documents. The *Constitution on the Liturgy, Sacrosanctum Concilium,* takes a standpoint nearly diametrically opposed to many liturgical rules and regulations valid before the Council. It emphasizes what was missing, such as participation by the community, spontaneity, and so forth, but does not speak so much about what was present, reverence for a transcendent God. Hence, present day liturgy is often strong in informality and intimacy, weak in reverence and praise to God.

The *Constitution on the Church in the Modern World, Gaudium et Spes,* reacts to a pessimistic view that saw little value in this creation and favored a spirituality that bypassed it or downrightly despised it. Therefore, the Constitution extols the world and stresses our duty to build the earth. But, if we do not perceive the dialectical nature of the Council's statement, we could fall into another extreme and seek salvation through the use of this creation, which would make the cross of Christ vain!

We have spoken at some length of these dialectical movements because we wanted to contrast the theological content of *Ordo paenitentiae* with that of some Council documents. The theological ideas of the *Ordo* are not dialectically conceived; they do not respond, still less do they react, to anything in the past. The *Ordo* corrects certain exaggerated and slanted opinions without saying so, but theologians of better vintage had been saying what is there for some time before Vatican Council II.

In these turbulent times, the *Ordo* intends to be a quiet event. It does not take a dialectical standpoint. By necessity, its contribution to the growth of our theological understanding is limited.

(e) Categories

Does the *Ordo* bring us new and more sophisticated categories?

From all that has been said up to this point, this question is relatively easy to answer. It does, in matters of liturgical celebration and pastoral care.

It does not, or hardly, in sacramental theology, and in

the related field of moral theology.

In sacramental theology, the traditional categories are reaffirmed right down to details: an individual confession is always necessary for absolution, except in the case of grave necessity. It is not said, but assumed, that the positive law which prescribes confession before communion for those aware of mortal sin continues to hold.

In matters concerning moral theology, the *Ordo* does not consider human sinfulness in any other way than in terms of mortal and venial sins. Yet, to give credit where it is due, the new rite for the reconciliation of individual penitents offers an opportunity to ascertain not only the sins of the penitent but his direction in life. The new rite is eminently suitable for a new discipline of penance that is closely allied with a moral theology that thinks primarily in terms of the direction of life of a Christian, rather than in the precise definition of sins.

* * * *

Our overall judgment of *Ordo paenitentiae* is that it is an important, practical step in the right direction. It does not offer many new insights theologically, but it introduces practical innovations that, through their success or failure, may lead to pioneering theological reflections. These, in their turn, may open new vistas, and give us more numerous and sophisticated categories than we have presently.

5

Fifth Question about the Future:
How Should Development Continue?

The sign of life is movement. Therefore, since the Church is a living body, it must continue to evolve toward the fulness of truth and an abundance of practical wisdom. Thus, at the end of our reflections, the question comes naturally: How can we participate in this movement? How can we contribute to such development?

To answer the question rightly, once again it is necessary to clarify its meaning. To contribute to the welfare of an evolving social body such as the Church is, is really to build for the future.

But, how can any mortal being foresee what is to come, and make his choices accordingly? We have had enough surprises in recent times to make us cautious, even taciturn, about forecasting what is to come.

Prophetic vision is not necessary. Our question is not really about the future, but about a present task. How can we lay good foundations for the future, in the present? Out of the evidence available here and now we should be able to plan. There lies our true and real contribution to the process of development.

The contribution could, and in the final analysis should, cover different fields such as sacramental and moral theology, liturgy and canon law, but we never intended such an extensive investigation in this study. We set a practical goal for ourselves: to find a method for the discovery of fitting structures and wise laws. To be faithful to this limited aim may well be the key to success! Therefore, we do not raise, still less do we solve, legitimate queries in theology such as "What is the meaning and role of confession made to God alone?", or "Could the sacrament ever be granted through confession to a layman?", or "What is the complex play between the powers of order and jurisdiction in granting absolution?'' These are all questions worthy of consideration in some new *summa theologica,* but that is not what we intended to write.

It follows that, in this last chapter, our answers must be modest and circumscribed. We are concerned with practical propositions which could be implemented presently—or soon, although not without changes in our liturgical norms and canonical discipline.[1]

In the preceding chapters, we followed a certain order. To understand the evolving Church, we first recorded external changes in their historical sequence. Then, we turned to the movements of ideas that take place behind external events. Finally, we reflected on the capacity of human persons and human communities to grow in knowledge, grace and wisdom.

Now we reverse the process. To find structures and norms that can help the Church to evolve, we focus first on persons; in them is the source of all reform. Then, we turn to ideas; they can shape and inspire external events. Finally, we come to external rules; they are necessary for the orderly life of a community.

(1) PERSONS: SOURCE OF ALL REFORMS

Fitting structures and wise laws can be produced only by qualified persons. This simple sentence has momentous consequences. Priority should be given to education.

---

[1]In other terms, we remain faithful to our goal. We try to propose fitting structures and wise laws *for our times.* Our question is: what is possible and permissible on doctrinal grounds? Often enough, presently valid liturgical norms and canonical laws allow less than what is possible and permissible on doctrinal grounds. When this is the case, we suggest an orderly change in the discipline.

There is a need for pioneers.

No progress in creating norms and structures, or anything else, is possible without raising new questions. But, to raise new and good questions is a difficult art; it must be learned.

Good questions are anchored in the known and they reach out into the unknown. They are like a boat that must depart from a precise point of the shore and go over the vast ocean to find land again, land which is perhaps dimly perceived in the mist or instinctively sensed by the navigator.

We know already that to raise new and good questions is to accept a risk. After all, all that we know with certainty is the port of our departure, not that of our arrival, if indeed there is an arrival. The early Christian communities knew that the Church had the power to forgive, but they had to ask how God's pardon should be signified. They found answers because they were compelled to search for them. Today we should ask if the signs we use could be extended and refined. This is a legitimate and practical issue.

No matter how much the *New Rite of Penance* may have given us, pioneers are needed nonetheless.

Only those can contribute to a historical process who enter into it.

To theologize means to reflect on God's mighty deeds in history. Some of those deeds have taken place in the past, and they live in the memory of the Christian community. Some of them are taking place in the present, and they can be known through faith, here and now. The Church was aware, from the beginning, that Christ had granted the power to forgive sin to the apostles. They reflected on this gift and worked out procedures to make it effective. Today, we know through faith that the gift has not faded; sins are still being forgiven. As we reflect, we can work out procedures different from the earlier ones.

But, past developments should teach us some caution for the present. We need not formulate norms and structures with any more absoluteness than the Church requires us to. Due to our own historical limitations, we cannot perceive all possible and permissible changes. We have not reached either the full truth or the abundance of wisdom that would foreclose progress.

Therefore, no matter how well we plan for the future, there will be a contingent and changeable element in our judgment. But this should not be an obstacle to the performance of our present task which is to contribute to development, not to settle all questions once for all.

Our horizons should expand.

Our horizons should expand in two ways: in seeing the impact of repentance on the whole life of the Church *and* in seeing the whole life of the Church as contributing to the development of the sacrament of penance.

The spirit of repentance is important for the internal life of the whole Church. We can have theologians who speak the language of angels, we can have seers to take us into the promised land of the future; but, if there is no repentance in the hearts of ordinary people, we have nothing, and will get nowhere. Many of our communities, small and large, are in need of repentance and healing, if not for the sins they have committed, certainly for lack of those good deeds they have omitted. There is a new role for the sacrament of penance.

The right development of the sacrament depends on other processes in the Church. The office of the presbyter ought to be understood better, more according to the Scriptures, in order to have priests to help those who are seeking pardon and healing. The sacrament, for full effectiveness, requires persons well-prepared in human learning and divine wisdom.

Further, the development of the sacrament of penance in any given age will be conditioned by the community's progress in understanding good and evil, right and wrong, that is, by their historical perception of Christian morality.

Philosophical reflections on our humanity, in particular on our own capacity to know, will inevitably influence our judgments at every level, whether they deal with our own limited world or with God's mighty deeds.

Finally, let us recall that the image of God we have sets the limits for our religious horizon. Because we are finite creatures, that image is finite, too, and conditioned in many ways. But, God himself is not conditioned; he is infinite. Therefore, the image we have of him can expand indefinitely. When it does, there are repercussions affecting our religious knowledge, including the knowledge of the sacrament of penance. That, too, can expand.

We should understand the role of opposing forces.

Every physical body that lives needs the creative energy that comes from dialectically opposed forces. A force which in itself could destroy the body is balanced by its opposite; the result is movement of life. We have a similar need in every social body; the realization of it gives a good point of departure for planning structures and norms. They must play their role dialectically.

A person intent on reform should be able to diagnose the balance of forces in the community and to inject new ones accordingly. For instance, if he sees that the sacrament of penance is used mostly for the reconciliation of individual penitents, he should ask how it could be applied for the healing of communities; if he perceives that the community has lost a healthy sense of sin, he should ask how they can be led to repentance, and so forth.

Every living body develops dialectically.

We must have the capacity to create new categories.

Let us suppose that there is a small house furnished in good taste, and in good order. Let us suppose that a magician touches the structure with his wand and makes all the outer walls expand. As this happens, every piece of furniture must be relocated. It will be necessary to rearrange the inside of the house and, conceivably, to bring in new objects to fill the place.

We use this example to illustrate a point. As our horizons expand, there is a need to rearrange our old categories and to create new ones to handle the broader field of reality revealed to us. As our universe expands, we need more sophisticated instruments to understand it.

The search for new structures and norms has already led us to a significant discovery. Our first and greatest need is to have persons who have the capacity to carry on the search and to recognize a find when it is there. Such persons must be ready to accept new questions as they come. They must have the humility to admit that their answers will be historically conditioned, and yet they must have the courage to provide strong remedies when weakness postulates them. They must have the ability to create new categories to respond to the needs of their expanded fields of knowledge and activity.

* * * *

The task awaiting those intent on reform is threefold, educational, legislative and doctrinal.

The *educational task* consists in providing a variety of information for our people, of giving them the models of right attitudes, so that they themselves can freely enter into a process of development. The *legislative task* lies in formulating intelligent norms for the administration of the sacrament of healing and forgiveness in the Church; there canonical and liturgical norms should blend harmoniously. The *doctrinal task* consists in critical theological reflections on our traditions and present needs so as to open the future for new thoughts, new ideas and new options for Christian values.

(2) EDUCATIONAL TASK

Awareness of Christian life.

We face a great challenge on the level of ideas. We need a more correct understanding of Christian life than we have now, and, by "we," we mean all: clergy, laity and religious. Christian life does not consist in a series of acts posited according to certain norms and laws; it consists in a sustained movement toward our God. The spring of this movement is generous love. No one can be truly Christian unless his desire is to love, that is, to give what he has—even himself—to God and to his fellow-men. This is a demanding process. The greatest obstacles to it are in counting, measuring, standing obstinately on our own rights.

Love poured into our hearts by the Spirit of God is our breath of life. Without it, life ceases. But, we receive this gift in vessels of clay—we have the awesome power to lose it.

Awareness of evil.

In preaching and teaching, in personal reflections on the word of God, we should honestly state the fact that this world has been torn apart by sin. The origins of every evil, such as the evil of war and violence, of manifest injustice and quiet denial of charity, are all there. This world, broken in so many ways, will not be healed until we understand that the roots of our problems are in human persons. They can be cured by God's grace only; that medicine alone can reach to the very source from where evil thoughts and deeds spring. Without being aware of sin and its role in this universe, we are not able to understand or to remedy the particular evils that are close to us. We easily attribute them to secondary causes only, and we are surprised when they do not go away after some superficial medicine is applied. No amount of social reform, necessary as it is, will bring us the kingdom of God; it can come only through the conversion of those who are given to evil, to God the source of all goodness.

Awareness of our own sinfulness.

To be aware of our own sinfulness is to understand ourselves better. The sinfulness is not just in our inclination to do something wrong, but in our power to violently destroy the life process in us by revolting against God. Our creaturely condition demands submission and obedience to our Creator. Our innate desire for the infinite brings us to wanting to be independent and free from him. That is the human condition which we all share.

The same can be stated in biblical terms. Mysteriously, in Adam, we all revolted and wanted to be like God. We wanted autonomy to decide what is right and what is wrong. Thus, we all tasted the forbidden fruit of disobedience (Cf. Rm 5). We are in need of healing as long as we live, all of us: little children whose minds are just opening up, grown-ups who seem to be masters of their own lives, old people who are preparing themselves to meet their Maker. We all need the healing power of the sacrament. No one is excepted.

Understanding Christian morality.

There is an enormous task of education to build up a new understanding of Christian morality which is primarily concerned with the movement of life and the direction it takes. The internal spring of this movement is love. Our fundamental duty is to keep love alive, this is the first and supreme commandment; or, to revive love in our hearts, if we have lost it, and thus to revive the movement of life. Such a conception of Christian life excludes petty casuistry that wants to combine the maximum of comfort with the minimum of effort in the service of the Lord. When the movement of life is failing, the sacrament of penance can strengthen it; when it has died, the sacrament can revive it.

Learning about the Christian way of life.

Every Christian wanting to live up to his vocation must listen to the word of God and must incorporate the moral teaching of Christ into his own life. This is an absolute duty. We are not called to follow the blind dictates of our conscience and, thus, to be slaves to obscurity. In fact, a blind conscience is an empty conscience; it cannot bind anyone. We are called to receive the luminous teaching of Christ. It tells us how to love and, consequently, how the movement of life can be sustained in us. It warns us away from attitudes and actions that may destroy it.

Appreciation of the sacrament.

In our educational effort, we must steadily uphold the value of the sacrament of reconciliation and healing. *Reconciliation* is necessary whenever a person has freely broken away from God, and from the community, through an offense so serious that it amounts to a full revolt against God and the Church's teaching, a "going out of" God's kingdom. Then, forgiveness must come through individual confession and absolution. *Healing* is useful for all because all are marked by sin, all need more strength in God's service.

Understanding the social dimension.

Education is certainly necessary to lead our people to the appreciation of the communal reception of the healing strength of penance. They should come to a realization that every sin is a social event; whoever offends God harms the community as well. They should become conscious that a whole community can sin through quiet, unarticulated conspiracy. The members' common judgments, dislikes, actions—all these can be marked by sin.

The role of private penance.

But, the appreciation of the social aspects of sin and pardon should not go to such an extreme that there is no room left for individual confessions, be it for reconciliation after serious failings, be it for the healing strength of the rite. Private confessions must be retained for all, although they can be optional for those who are not aware of a fundamental break with God.

Understanding of sin.

A most difficult, but indispensable, task in education is to help our people to understand correctly the nature of sin: it is the breakdown of the movement toward God. They should know that not all that is seriously harmful is necessarily fatal; yet, what is not fatal can be seriously harmful.

The Catholic community, at present, is conditioned by the classical division of sin into mortal and venial; they can hardly think in any other way. An innocent speaker may not even have finished saying that not all serious sins are mortal, when part of the audience already concludes that they are allowed—nay, virtuous. Such a reaction is absurd but understandable. It springs from a philosophy in which the primary concern is to define the essential quality of the act. A profitable dialogue, as opposed to useless arguments, can be built up only by going back to the foundations. The differences in conceiving morality have their origins in different cognitional theories.

* * * *

The educational task can be summed up by saying that we must become, and remain, aware that as each one of us is marked by sin, so is the whole community—the universal Church, particular churches, and groups of Christians in whatever way they come together. It follows that the life of Christians, of individuals and of groups, must be an ongoing conversion.[2]

There is no better way of promoting this process than the judicious use of the sacrament of penance. Of this we speak in the next section.

(3) LEGISLATIVE TASK

Because the Christian community is marked by sin, its ordinary way of life should be marked by repentance. Intense use of the sacrament of penance can be an expression of this repentance, and can sustain it. Wise legislation can promote such use.

---

[2]The term "conversion" has been used so much in recent years that it has become a cliché which we have heard over and over again. We must go through a radical conversion.

The truth of the matter is that the vast majority of Christians grow in grace and wisdom gently, slowly, and often painfully. Dramatic conversions such as Paul's and Augustine's are relatively rare. Ordinary preaching and teaching should be concerned with fostering the process of life, that is growth and expansion in understanding and love. This can be called a steady turning toward God, an ongoing conversion.

General absolution.

Penance services for several penitents with general absolution could be allowed with greater facility. In fact, they should be allowed whenever there is no doctrinal objection against them and there are good pastoral reasons to have them.

Penitential services with general absolution could be introduced and held regularly for groups of some natural unity. A group of children of the same age is a good example. As soon as the minds of the children begin to open up and they can distinguish good from evil, that is, as soon as they begin to operate with some fractional freedom proportionate to their age, the sacrament of penance could be offered to them through services adjusted to their intelligence. Through simple homilies, they could be shown how God loves them and works in their hearts, and how they can destroy his love through selfishness. They should be taught to choose what is right, and to repent if they have done wrong. The educative value of the frequent reception of the sacrament, right in the beginning of their conscious life, would be great. They would experience God's healing power just at the right time—when they are beginning to give a direction to their own lives.[3]

---

[3]Once such penitential services are offered to children, the widely disputed issue of what should come first, confession or communion, loses its importance. Surely, children should be taught to repent as soon as, in their own little way, they can yield to evil. The healing gift of the sacrament should be offered to them right from that age, but not necessarily in the form of individual confession. Group services can be far more suitable for them. They are ready to partake in the Eucharist around the same time.

Few moral theologians would admit, today, that a child of seven years or about that age, could sin "mortally." If he cannot, he is not bound

Penitential services with common absolution could be held, also, for communities of religious sisters and brothers, or for groups of priests and seminarians. With such groups there is not a need to stress individual reconciliation, since no one is likely to be there if he is in the state of revolt against God. But, there is every need to call them all to repentance, and to invite them to accept the healing gift of the sacrament.

Such services could restore and promote the regular reception of the sacrament in religious communities, in seminaries, and among priests. The present situation is not a healthy one. Not only has access to the sacrament of penance declined in communities of religious and priests (as well as among the faithful), but their spirit of penance has suffered from gradual erosion. It is an illusion to think that frequent confessions on the old pattern will be resumed, nor does the very elaborate nature of the new pattern encourage such practice. Therefore, the only way of restoring the use of the sacrament is to introduce community services with general absolution.

Such a new discipline could be extended further. A parish could hold regular penitential services with general absolution for those who desire to participate in them. It would be an opportunity for an examination of the conscience of the parish. The priest could raise pertinent questions concerning the way of life of the community, questions that could make them aware of their common sins and omissions, and might bring them to repentance. He

by any of our laws to go to confession. The reason is simple and decisive: the Council of Trent demands yearly confession only from those who know themselves to be guilty of "mortal" sin. Children should have the same liberties as adults.

could ask them, for instance, whether in their thinking, speaking and acting, they show forth the Christian ideal of justice and charity. If not, how should they repent and change? The local churches would have a powerful instrument of renewal in such sacramental services.

Further, whenever there is a meeting of the bishop with his priests, they could, all together, repent of their wrong deeds and omissions, and promise God to serve him and his people better. Then, they all should receive the sacrament of healing. The celebration of the Eucharist would follow quite naturally. *There* would be an experience of unity!

In fact, whenever a group of Christians meet for some specific purpose, for instance a retreat, they could ask for and obtain God's mercy in common, and obtain forgiveness in common, too. As the Eucharist is a community celebration, so would the sacrament of penance be.[4]

A strong objection to such new discipline can be heard: it would introduce divisions into the community. After all, we have affirmed that those who have broken away from God and from the community must receive the sacrament of reconciliation individually. It follows that there would be two distinct groups of Christians only too visible, those who go to confession and those who do not—the sinners and the innocents!

The objection is not as strong as it appears. For cen-

---

[4]We are aware of various statements issued by the Holy See concerning general sacramental absolution (see the report, "General Sacramental Absolution," in THE JURIST, vol. 37 [1977] pp. 180-182). While they contain information about the mind of the legislator, they do not amount to legislation.

turies, we have held to the rule that only those who are in
the state of grace should receive communion. There are
those who go to communion and those who do not. Yet,
the division—if we can speak of one—is handled with
discretion by every community. There is a general respect
for the conscience of each, and it is not even good manners
to speak about who received communion and who did not.
We should trust, again, the good sense of our people. Once
instructed properly, they would show the same discretion
and tact regarding penance as they have so firmly shown
concerning the Eucharist.

People should understand clearly that the opportunity
for private confession is always there, for everybody. It is a
forum of reconciliation and spiritual direction. They
should know, also, that whenever a son has gone out of the
house of his father and "squandered his property in loose
living" (Lk 15:13), he must ask for readmission personally.
Those who have remained faithful and have not gone out
of their father's house, but are in need of healing, can
receive the remedy the sacrament brings through public admission of their sinfulness and general absolution. As a
matter of fact, we think that many who are not in need of
being reconciled individually would still seek the quiet
privacy of individual confession for both spiritual direction and absolution.

The issue of confession before communion.

Since there is, today, a general revision of the laws of the
Church, the question should be raised as to whether or not
the Tridentine law that prescribes confession before communion, for all those who feel guilty of mortal sin, should

be kept (cf. *Conc. Tridentinum, sessio* 13, canon 11; Denzinger-Schoenmetzer, ed. 34, 1661; *Codex Iuris Canonici,* canon 856).

In favor of keeping the law is the fact that it brings some order and clarity into the life of the community; it brings peace to individual consciences; also, it upholds a certain respect for the Eucharist.

All the intended results are excellent. Yet, someone may ask if they should be obtained through legislation or if they could be achieved through general teaching and pastoral care. The answer may not be as clear as we would like it to be. Certainly there are strong theological reasons to suggest a general obligation to go to the sacrament of reconciliation before partaking in the Eucharist. Is this obligation so strong that the present law adds nothing to it, but is merely the promulgation of what is the duty of every repentant sinner? If so, can people be made aware of this duty without legislating about it?

We are inclined to think that, in ordinary circumstances, there is a binding duty to seek reconciliation through confession and absolution, before partaking in the Eucharist. The law does no more than to say explicitly what our implicit common belief is. If we add that mortal sins may not be as frequent as many manuals claim them to be, but that when they occur they extinguish life, a theology which upholds the duty to obtain reconciliation before Eucharistic communion makes good sense, indeed—to the point that nothing else makes sense.

Power to absolve.

Legislation concerning the faculties of priests to hear confessions is in sore need of reform. The present regulations are unsatisfactory. With easy travel from one diocese to another, in fact from one country to another, it no longer makes sense to restrict the capacity to hear confessions to the priest's own diocese. Besides, the faithful do not know, still less do they understand, such restrictive norms; consequently, embarrassing situations arise all too frequently. To say that they should be taken care of by "common error" or some other legal device is to make a mockery of our laws. Radically new and well-adjusted norms are needed, if not for the sake of priests, certainly for the benefit of the faithful.

This issue has been looked upon too much from the point of view of upholding the right of the ordinary to grant faculties, and not enough from the point of view of the unknown penitent who needs help. The right principle for designing new legislation should aim to take care of the penitent first. Whenever someone repents and wants to receive the sacrament, he should be able to receive it without delay from any priest of his choice who is in good standing with his own ordinary.[5]

It may surprise many to hear that the Church in the Middle Ages had a much broader approach to the issue of the power to absolve than it has today. True, Lateran Council

---

[5]True, the ordinary has the right to grant faculties to priests to hear confessions, but, on the whole, ordinaries have often been more cautious than is warranted by pastoral need, and more so in the United States than in Europe. If every American bishop just imitated the generous attitude of the diocese of Rome in granting faculties to traveling priests, we would have no problem. Presently, we do have problems in America. Many traveling priests simply rely on real or imaginary legal devices such as common error, doubt of fact or doubt of law, and presume that the Church tacitly supplies them with jurisdiction. There is really no need for such devices. Good laws agreed on by the bishops of the country could easily take care of the situation.

IV in 1215 decreed that everyone of the faithful should confess his sins yearly to his own priest, *proprio sacerdoti,* but a custom developed of assuming tacit delegation whenever someone chose another priest. After the Council of Trent, a double requirement was gradually imposed on priests. They had to be approved for confessions, mainly on the basis of their knowledge of moral theology; and then, they had to obtain faculties, either through the machinery of the law or the personal act of the bishop. Someone may well be approved for confessions, today, and yet have no power to forgive sins.

Times have changed. The Church has more to gain by a generous policy of making the sacred signs of forgiveness available than by restricting them for the sake of organizational clarity.

In those countries where the episcopal conferences have effectively taken care of this problem, the pattern of the law is simple. Each bishop grants faculties to a priest who arrives in another diocese than his own, for a temporary stay, provided that the priest has faculties from his own ordinary. This rule takes care of situations that arise from traveling, yet the bishop retains his authority over ordinary pastoral care.

If the use of general absolution is extended, the question of faculties will become a more delicate one. It will not be an issue of granting absolution privately, but of celebrating liturgy publicly. It is fair and just that public penance services with general absolution, apart from cases of emergency, should be presided over by those priests only who hold faculties from the local ordinary.

Annual confession.

Then there is the law of Lateran Council IV in 1215 imposing the duty of annual confession, binding, as often assumed, under mortal sin (cf. D-Sch. 812; *Codex Iuris Canonici,* can. 906).[6] Should it be retained? This is a distinct issue from that of confession before communion.

The strongest argument in favor is that, in many cases, the law seemingly worked—it brought the faithful to the confessional.

On the other hand, it can be asked if the same result could not be obtained by intense pastoral work. There seems to be something absurd in imposing an obligation under mortal sin, on someone who is already in mortal sin! Should mercy be imposed through such a deterrent?

* * * *

[6]No doubt, the reader has noticed our careful formulation, "binding, as often assumed, under mortal sin." There are momentous theological issues lurking in the background. Let us just point to them.

The pope, the supreme and virtually the only legislator for the universal Church, certainly has the radical power to pronounce over an issue of moral theology. The question is does he want to determine the gravity of the offense with full apostolic authority when he imposes a grave obligation through legislation; or, is it more reasonable to say that he does not intend to give any kind of definition of gravity, but leaves it to the theologians to work out the seriousness of an act of disobedience to the law.

In other terms, when the legislator states that the law binds gravely, *sub gravi,* it should be received by all as a grave obligation. But, no one is entitled to assume easily that the law contains a precise definition of gravity in the sense of "mortal." When the pope promulgates a disciplinary law, it is not immediately evident that he wants to decide the doctrinal issue of the gravity of an offense. Disobedience to the law, of course, can have very serious consequences, without implying a death sentence.

Let us, now, sum up the proposed new norms for the sacrament of penance:

(1) In ordinary circumstances, those who have broken away from God and from the community must be reconciled individually; that is, they must go to confession.

(2) All those who wish to receive the sacrament of penance individually have a right to do so; that is, all may go to confession.[7]

(3) The sacrament of penance with general absolution should be offered regularly to communities such as religious communities, schools, parishes, sick persons in hospitals.

(4) Faculties for priests, including those from other dioceses, for the internal forum, *in foro conscientiae,* should be extended by laws, general and particular; for the external forum, *in foro externo,* especially for general absolution, should be granted by the bishop.

As always, good legislation is marked by restraint. These norms are deceptively few, but they would reach far. Whatever can be obtained by exhortation, pastoral help and individual guidance should not be imposed by laws.

(4) DOCTRINAL TASK

Every good book on theology is open-ended. It must be so; it deals with mysteries. No matter how much the author

---

[7]At this point, we would like to insert another canon: all those who wish to receive the sacrament of penance anonymously have a right to do so. This is clearly against the letter, and perhaps even the spirit, of the new rite of penance, yet it is a method that has proved itself many times over. The good that comes from it outweighs its liturgical deficiencies. Who of us has not seen, at one time or another, the crowd of penitents which a compassionate blind priest can attract!

has discovered, there is more. This book is not an exception. It reports on the present state of our evolving understanding. Others will come with new insights and will carry on the process toward the unreachable goal: the fulness of truth.

The purpose of the following paragraphs is precisely to show how much this book is open-ended, and how much more reflection is needed to progress in the understanding of the sacrament of penance, and in the understanding of Christian morality that is so closely related to it.

We were quite definite when we spoke about educational proposals and legislative tasks. There we stated our conclusions. We cannot be so definite about many points of doctrine. Here we can state our questions. Even so, they have a limited scope: to serve as examples of the type of problems which must be examined and solved to a reasonable degree before those firm doctrinal conclusions can be reached that will determine, in so many ways, the process of forgiveness—the rites of the dispensation of pardon—in the Church.

We are really not doing anything else than presenting the reader with a list of disputed questions—a fitting end to a book of this style.

Good questions should start from the known. So, as a convenient device, we anchor our questions in the text of canon 7 of the fourteenth session of the Council of Trent in 1551. To this day, the understanding of the sacrament of penance, and even of moral theology, is closely bound to that canon. Nearly every word in it can serve as a springboard for further reflection. Of course, we do not suggest that no work has been done on this text, but that full answers to our questions are not available as yet.

The Fathers of the Council of Trent "determined" that

Whoever says that in the sacrament of penance it is
not necessary, according to divine law, for the remission of sins, to confess all and every mortal sin that
the memory recalls through due and diligent reflection,

including occult sins and sins against the last two of
the ten commandments,

including circumstances that change the classification
(species) of sin;

further, [*whoever says*] that confession is useful only
for the instruction and consolation of the penitent,
and that once it was done only in view of the imposition of canonical penance;

or, whoever says that those who strive to confess all
their sins do not want to leave anything, for pardon,
to the divine mercy; or, that it is not permitted to confess venial sins,

be such a person anathema (Denzinger-
Schoenmetzer, ed. 34, 1707).

*Let us begin with the closing words of the canon:
anathema sit, "be cursed" in literal translation. What is
the meaning of this condemnation? Does it mean that
every single clause in the canon is of the same doctrinal
value; or, does it allow for different doctrinal weights in so
many clauses? If so, what is the precise weight of each
clause?

Further, what was the intention of the Fathers: did they

want to declare those who denied all or part of the canon heretics; or, did they intend to denounce them as dangerous persons, threatening the peace and unity of the community? In other terms, how far is the condemnation doctrinal, how far is it disciplinary?

*To confess is said to be *necessarium,* "necessary," for the remission of mortal sin. What is the meaning of "necessary"? It is certainly not an absolute necessity that allows no exceptions, since the long-standing tradition of the Church is that, in case of mortal danger, there is always an exception and, to obtain God's pardon, confession is not necessary. So the text obviously refers to ordinary circumstances. But, just what are those ordinary circumstances? How can they be known and defined with some precision? The tradition is far from being clear on this point.

What kind of confession was necessary in the Mediterranean system? Certainly not the kind that we know today. There is little doubt historically (*pace* the Fathers of Trent) that, in the Irish pattern, detailed confession of sins was necessary in order to enable the priest to determine the amount of satisfaction. But most, if not all, satisfactions imposed today are more nominal than real. What is the impact, if any, of this gradual development on the rule that the confession of sins is necessary? As long as the meaning of our tradition has not been clarified, in one way or another, it is difficult to draw conclusions for our times.

*Such necessity is imposed *iure divino,* "by divine right," meaning, seemingly, a law revealed by God. We should know where and how it has been revealed. How did the Church become aware of this revelation? Besides, what does divine right mean in this particular context? A command that the Church cannot touch, or a command that it can somehow interpret and modify? There are studies on this issue but, as yet, there is no firm conclusion.

Besides, there is the epistemological issue: assuming that there is a divine law, how far does our capacity to know it extend?

*What is the meaning of *confiteri,* "to confess"? Clearly, it means at least that the sinner professes himself a sinner before the Church. He submits himself to the Church. He declares his faith in the hidden power to forgive sins present in the community and administered by its consecrated ministers. But, ever since the beginning of the Irish tradition, "to confess" has meant more; it has meant the specific enumeration of sins, often quite irrespective of their gravity.

*What is the meaning of *peccatum grave,* "mortal sin"? On this point, moral theology is in full fermentation. It is certainly breaking away from the concept as it appears in manuals of pre-Vatican II vintage. To find the correct answer, we should know, first, how far, if at all, the Council of Trent canonized any definition of mortal sin. There is no evidence that it did. Obviously, the extent of the application of canon 7 depends on the understanding of mortal sin.

It would be silly to conclude, though, that because the Council did not define authoritatively what mortal sin is, no such sin exists. The Christian community has never hesitated about its possibility; the tradition has shifted a great deal about its extension.

*What is the dialectical stance at the Council of Trent? How far are its statements dialectical responses to Protestant positions as the Council understood them? How far are they detached determinations, with precision and accuracy, of Catholic belief? The answers to the questions will come only slowly.

*There is the problem of *satisfactio,* "satisfaction." Much of the balance of the sacrament, in both the Mediterranean and Irish systems, depended on the right measure of satisfaction; its gravity had to be in proportion to the offense. Post-Tridentine theologians built up an argument for detailed confession precisely from the need of assessing the satisfaction. But, who can deny that satisfaction, today, has become a small devotional exercise with little or no relation to the gravity of the offense. The vocabulary is carried on from earlier ages. The need to impose satisfaction proportionate to the offense is firmly stated. Yet, who can seriously pretend that "five 'Our Fathers' and five 'Hail Marys' " is proportionate, in any way, to an offense that deserved eternal damnation? The doctrine that sustained satisfaction has certainly been eroded.

* * * *

Many more disputed questions could be listed, originating in the Council of Trent or elsewhere, but our intention was to show by examples how much more research and reflection need to be done. We do have many good questions, and good theology should know how to live with questions. There is no need to cling to solutions that cannot stand up to rigorous critical examination.

Good questions will, eventually, bring us good answers. Due to them, we shall be all the closer to the truth.[8]

[8]Vatican Council II put it beautifully—the judgment of the Church must mature:

> But, since holy Scripture must be read and interpreted according to the same Spirit by whom it was written, no less serious attention must be given to the content and unity of the whole of Scripture, if the meaning of the sacred texts is to be correctly brought to light. The living tradition of the whole Church must be taken into account along with the harmony which exists between elements of the faith. It is the task of exegetes to work according to these rules toward a better understanding and explanation of the meaning of sacred Scripture, so that through preparatory study *the judgment of the Church may mature (Constitution on Divine Revelation, Dei Verbum,* #12; [emphasis ours]).

Parting Words

A book of this nature should not have a conclusion. It is really about the journey of a pilgrim people, and they are still on the march. Even if our present observations and reflections come to an end, the Church continues to evolve, and God's mercy to unfold.

In the beginning, we stated our purpose: to find a good method for discovering fitting structures and wise laws. On this last page of the book, let us state firmly that there is another task to be performed.

We must reflect on our image of God. There is much in that image that is true, since we have received it from Jesus. There is much in it that is our own creation, and therefore ought to be corrected. As we come to a deeper knowledge of God and greater love of him, we shall understand more fully the demands of Christian life and the mystery of mercy.

The key to the discovery of fitting structures and wise laws is in knowing God better and loving him more.

So, the journey must go on.

Selected and Annotated Bibliography

The purpose of these notes is twofold: to give an account of our own background and to help the reader to further study.

Some books on the Church and the sacrament of penance:

Alszeghy, Zoltán and Flick, Maurizio.
Il sacramento della riconciliazione.
Torino: Marietti, 1976.

A concise history with thoughtful reflections.

Amann, E. *et al.*
"Pénitence." *Dictionnaire de théologie catholique,* vol. 12, cols. 722-1138.
Paris: Letouzey, 1933.

A thoroughly documented overall study on the sacrament of penance.

Anciaux, Paul.
Le sacrament de la pénitence.
Louvain: Nauwelaerts, 1963.

A textbook that shows strong awareness of history and contains reflections from a fundamentally classical point of view.

Chirico, Peter.
Infallibility: The Crossroads of Doctrine.
Kansas City: Sheed Andrews and McMeel, 1977.

This book is a remarkable attempt to bring understanding into the issue of the development of doctrine or, more correctly, the development of Christian persons who eventually may come to the infallible understanding of a point of doctrine.

Congar, Yves.
Vraie et fausse réforme dans l'église.
Paris: Cerf, 1969.

This book was first published in 1950. Much reform has taken place in the Church since! The core content of the book is as valid as ever; the rest can be read as interesting historical documentation.

Delhaye, Philippe.
The Christian Conscience.
Translated from the French by Charles U. Quinn.
New York: Desclée, 1968.

A systematic treatise on conscience. Limited by its all-embracing pattern, it displays a keen sense for history and evolution. It gives abundant bibliographical references.

Dulles, Avery R.
The Resilient Church: the Necessity and Limits of Adaptation.
Garden City: Doubleday, 1977.

This book is on developments since Vatican Council II. The author deals with a number of vital issues, such as the Church's mission, development of dogma, *sensus fidelium,* primacy and others. It can be very enlightening for non-Americans about the American theological scene.

Dussaut, Louis.
L'Eucharistie. Pâque de toute la vie.
Paris: Cerf, 1972.

The author proposes significant changes in the

Eucharistic celebration, but he grounds his proposals in a thorough examination of our traditions. The knowledge of what our Christian ancestors believed, knew and did may free us for more significant changes than many recent speculations. His approach is akin to the method we propose.

Galtier, Paul.
L'Église et la rémission des péchés aux premiers siècles.
Paris: Beauchesne, 1932.

Rich and detailed documentation; less strong in hermeneutical interpretation.

Gemeinsame Synode der Bistuemer in der Bundesrepublik Deutschland.
Freiburg: Herder, 1976 (vol. 1), 1977 (vol. 2).

The churches of Western Germany preparing for action through a national synod. A model of reflective search for fitting structures and wise norms in this post-conciliar period.

Gonzalez del Valle, José M.
El sacramento de la penitencia.
Pamplona: Universidad de Navarra, 1972.

The author's interest is in the juridical aspects of penance that, in his judgment, have not been sufficiently explored either historically or systematically. He does his investigations by focusing on different themes such as the scope of penance, jurisdiction, satisfaction, secrecy, reservation, and so forth. In his conclusion, he offers thirteen rules for the "juridical reconstruction" of the sacrament of penance.

Hainz, Josef.
Kirche im Werden.
Muenchen: Schoeningh, 1976.

Thirteen essays on the themes of office and community in the New Testament. Enlightening studies on the emergence and first development of some of our ecclesiastical institutions.

Liturgie et rémission des péchés. Conferences Saint-Serge, XXe Semaine d'Etudes Liturgiques.
Roma: Edizioni Liturgiche, 1975.

This is a collection of seventeen papers given during the "Twentieth Week of Liturgical Studies, Conferences of St. Serge," held in Paris in 1973. The theme of the convention was "Liturgy and the Forgiveness of Sins." Some of the studies about penitential life in the Orthodox Church are especially informative.

Lossky, Vladimir.
In the Image and Likeness of God.
New York: St. Vladimir's Seminary Press, 1974.

The oriental tradition: the more we understand something of God's mystery, the more we realize man's dignity. There is a great deal in this book about the holy and strong God who is full of mercy: "But let us not forget, in the presence of the awesome countenance of Christ the Judge, that the supreme prerogative of a King is mercy" (p. 227).

Moltmann, Juergen.
The Church in the Power of the Spirit.
New York: Harper & Row, 1975.

> The book is on the power of the Spirit in the historical
> Church which is developing in the midst of changing
> cultures. A work of exceptional importance for
> ecumenical understanding among the Christian
> churches.

Monden, Louis.
Sin, Liberty and Law.
Translated by Joseph Donceel.
New York: Sheed and Ward, 1965.

> A small classic that has had much influence although
> the thoughts of theologians have progressed a great
> deal since its publication. It gives good
> bibliographical references to writings between the end
> of the second World War and the beginning of
> Vatican II. It does not end with a conclusion, but
> with a question. Such works often endure—even if
> they are short, as this book is.

Muehlen, Heribert.
Der Heilige Geist als Person.
Muenster: Aschendorff, 1963.

> Faith in the Holy Spirit seeks understanding—a
> thoughtful synthesis deeply rooted in the Scriptures.
> To understand development in the Church, it is
> necessary to seek understanding of the presence of the
> Spirit within it.

———

Una Mystica Persona.
Muenchen: Schoeningh, 1967.

A book of unusual depth about the Church. It contains extensive reflections on biblical traditions and careful explanations of the texts of Vatican Council II. It might be the best we have in modern systematic theology.

Ordo paenitentiae. Editio typica.
Typis Polyglottis Vaticanis, 1973.

The official Latin text.

Osborne, Kenan, *et al.*
Committee Report: The Renewal of the Sacrament of Penance.
The Catholic Theological Society of America, 1975.

This report contains good historical material; it considers modern needs and makes recommendations. Although somewhat uneven in parts, as a whole it is an important contribution. Under one aspect it is indispensable: it contains a virtually complete bibliography on penance from 1965 to 1972. Regrettably, no annotations or critical evaluations are added to the titles.

Palmer, Paul F.
Sacraments and Forgiveness. Sources of Christian Theology, vol. 2.
Westminster, MD: Newman, 1959.

A collection of documents, in English translation, with short commentaries.

Pianazzi, G. and Triacca, A., eds.
Sacramento della Penitenza.
Zuerich: Pas, 1974.

> A symposium of papers given at a convention for
> priests and educators, at the Pontifical Salesian
> University in Rome. The essays, explicitly or implicit-
> ly, are a documentation of the present fermentation.
> They show that the problems are very similar from
> one part of the world to another. The themes dis-
> cussed in Italy are boiling issues in America—or
> elsewhere. A paragraph from the introductory study
> by Zoltán Alszeghy illustrates this:
>> Ecclesiastical penance is an evolutive [*dynamic*]
>> structure. In it, one indispensable aspect of the
>> life of the Church takes shape in forms that are
>> always new, in forms that respond to the
>> historical and cultural circumstances in which
>> the Church lives. Now, the life of an evolutive
>> structure consists in a permanent fundamental
>> theme (the "formal" element) that changes con-
>> tinuously, organically, in every one of its com-
>> ponent parts (the "material" elements) (p. 9).

Poschmann, Bernhard.
Penance and the Anointing of the Sick.
Translated by Francis Courtney.
New York: Herder and Herder, 1964.

> One of the best overall histories on the sacrament of
> penance available in English. The German original
> was published in 1951. The work is rich in factual in-
> formation; it does not, however, display a deep sen-
> sitivity for the problems of development and evolu-
> tion.

Rahner, Karl.
Foundations of Christian Faith.
New York: Seabury, 1978.
Theological Investigations, vol. 2.
Baltimore: Helicon Press, 1963.

Rahner has made a significant contribution to the understanding of the "sinful" Church and the meaning and use of the sacrament of penance. His older writings (such as some of those on penance) can be better understood in the light of his recent *summa.*

Sala, Giovanni B.
Dogma e storia.
Bologna: Edizioni Dehoniane, 1976.

The core of the book is on the pilgrim Church in the deepest sense, the developing understanding of the word of God in the Christian community. This core is introduced by an explanation of epistemological foundations. It is followed by a demonstration of the historical character of dogma in the *Mysterium ecclesiae.*

Taylor, Michael J., ed.
The Mystery of Sin and Forgiveness.
New York: Alba House, 1970.

A re-publication, in English, of fourteen essays published in the 1960's in theological journals. The authors are mostly theologians of reputation. They deal with the historical, doctrinal and pastoral aspects of the sacrament. The majority of the essays can serve well as introductions into the problems.

Tentler, Thomas N.
Sin and Confession on the Eve of the Reformation.
Princeton: Princeton University Press, 1977.

A vast collection of detailed information concerning
the understanding of sin and penitential practices on
the eve of the Reformation. However, the author's
understanding of deeper theological issues in no way
matches his industry in collecting data from all
sources, scientific and popular. The overall picture is
one of a limited, if not distorted, presentation of
Christian faith and practice.

Todd, John M.
Problems of Authority.
Baltimore: Helicon, 1962.

A collection of essays, some dated, some still fresh.
They discuss the living authorities in the Church: the
word of God, the Holy Spirit, the teaching and governing power of the bishops. Peter Fransen's contribution, "The Authority of the Councils," is highly rele-
vant for the interpretation of conciliar texts, cf. the
last pages in our book about the Council of Trent.

Vogel, Cyrille.
Le pécheur et la pénitence dans l'église ancienne.
Paris: Cerf, 1966.
Le pécheur et la pénitence au Moyen Âge.
Paris: Cerf, 1969.

The two small volumes contain a collection of
selected sources translated into French and com-
mented on by Cyrille Vogel. The documents are
judiciously chosen. The author lets them speak for
themselves for the most part, adding short and con-

cise, but much to the point, observations. He has a good understanding of changes and developments.

Wasserschleben, Hermann
Die Bussordnungen der abendländischer Kirche.
Graz: Akademische Druckanstalt, 1958. (Reprint of 1851 edition).

A classical reference book, widely used ever since its publication.

Some books on epistemology, hermeneutics and kindred issues:

Arnheim, Rudolph.
Visual Thinking.
Berkeley: University of California Press, 1969.

The former professor of psychology of art at Harvard became interested in the art of thinking. He wrestles, in his own way, with the problem that has kept philosophers reflecting ever since the early Greek periods: the relationship between sense perception and understanding. Although he is not a metaphysician, his book is an interesting and illustrative commentary on the scholastic saying, *nihil est in intellectu quod non fuit in sensu*; there is nothing in the mind that has not passed somehow through the senses.

Bastian, Hans-Dieter.
Theologie der Frage.
Muenchen: Kaiser, 1969.

The main interest of the author is in the role that questions play in theology. But, the book is really a series of reflections on the role of questions in philosophy, psychology, anthropology, sociology, biblical studies—even preaching. An original and refreshing study.

Bent, Charles N.
Interpreting the Doctrine of God.
New York: Paulist Press, 1969.

The theme of the book is development of Christian doctrine and, by implication, development of a cognitional relationship between God and man. The thoughts of four theologians—Dewart, Newman, Rahner and Lonergan—are presented and analyzed. There is a good list of books and articles on development of doctrine.

Bronowski, Jacob.
The Ascent of Man.
Boston: Little, Brown and Co., 1973.

The story of the ascent of man, as told by Bronowski, is a fine illustration of what Maréchal called *le dynamisme de l'intelligence,* the dynamic nature of the mind, or our restless quest for knowledge.

––––

A Sense of the Future.
Cambridge, MA: MIT Press, 1977.

A collection of articles written over a period of twenty-five years. They witness the search of a scientist not only for the understanding of the material world, but of man himself. Inevitably, he faces the issue of the process of understanding and choice of values. Bronowski, in his own way, has struggled with many issues that theologians must face today; after all, questions about the ultimate reality are not that much different for a scientist and a theologian.

Clark, Kenneth.
Civilisation.
New York: Harper & Row, 1969.

This book makes even more interesting reading if we recall that civilizations are born, first, in the mind of man, and that man himself is an evolving being with an increasing capacity to create civilizations.

Clark, Ronald W.
Einstein: The Life and Times.
New York: World, 1971.

To understand the mind of an explorer and discoverer, it is always necessary to know something about his life and the times in which he lived.

de Finance, Joseph.
L'affrontement de l'autre.
Roma: Università Gregoriana, 1973.

Philosophical reflections that take for their point of departure the unfolding of the activity of one human person toward another person. There is much in this book that helps us to understand how human community evolves and develops. Its focus on action is a good counterbalance to so many other philosophies that focus nearly exclusively on knowledge.

Dolle, Jean-Marie.
Pour comprendre Jean Piaget.
Toulouse: Privat, 1974.

It has been said many times that Piaget is the explorer
of the world of intelligence as Freud was the explorer
of the world of emotions. Of the two, Piaget is the
more difficult to understand. Here we have a good
presentation of both his empirical research and his
penetrating reflections.

In our last chapter, we speak of the need for education in the Christian community, that is, of the need
to lead Christians to a better understanding of our
way of life. Some of Piaget's principles could be of
help in this process.

Dulles, Avery.
The Survival of Dogma.
Garden City: Doubleday, 1971.

The Christian realities of faith, teaching authority
and dogma, says the author, undergo a discontinuous
"quantum leap" each time the culture, in which
Christianity is embedded, passes into a new phase.
Twelve essays explicitate this thesis.

We could press the issue further and say that,
whenever culture passes into a new phase, Christians
undergo a discontinuous "quantum leap" in their
own development and come to see the same realities
in a new way.

Dunne, John S.
The Reasons of the Heart.
New York: Macmillan, 1978.

The most recent work of the author. It would be difficult to determine the literary form of his writings.

They are long reflective essays about the ultimate problems of man. Dunne goes out to explore new worlds beyond the small valley of our everyday existence.

Einstein, Albert.
Relativity: The Special and the General Theory.
Authorised translation by Robert W. Lawson.
New York: Crown, 1961.

Einstein's discovery of the laws of relativity was, also, a discovery in the process of knowing, a kind of modern version of the discovery of the mind that took place at the dawn of Greek philosophy. Besides, his method of explaining the most abstract theories through down-to-earth examples can serve as inspiration to any writer concerned with the relation between theory and practice. Just to avoid any misunderstanding, let us recall that the theory of relativity is concerned with finding out the true state of the universe as far as possible, not with making everything relative. But the true state of things can never be even approximately known unless the position of the observer enters into the basic equation of all operations. There is plenty of inspiration in Einstein's work for theologians, even if there are no literal applications.

Gadamer, Hans-Georg.
Truth and Method.
New York: Seabury, 1975.

A thorough and extensive inquiry into the problems of hermeneutics, with special reference to theology.

Hamilton, Edith and Cairns, Huntington, eds.
Plato: The Collected Dialogues.
Princeton: Princeton University Press, 1961.

For the sake of keeping alive in ourselves the method of learning through questions, we strongly suggest a re-reading of some of these dialogues.

Kaspar, Walter.
Die Methoden in Dogmatik. Einheit und Vielheit.
Muenchen: Koesel, 1967.

In a short essay, the author shows the need for new theological method.

Lonergan, Bernard.
Insight: A Study of Human Understanding.
London: Longmans, 1957.
Method in Theology.
New York: Herder and Herder, 1972.

Lonergan is a participant in that philosophical discourse about human knowledge that has gone on ever since Socrates raised his questions in Athens, Aquinas held his disputations in Paris, and Kant lectured in Koenigsberg. Lonergan is familiar with their problems, but he offers his own answers to epistemological and cognitional questions. His insights are having a deep impact on theology. There is an abundant literature, already, discussing his positions.

Malevez, Léopold.
Pour une théologie de la foi.
Paris: Desclée De Brouwer, 1969.

A book rich in insights which are proposed with great *finesse.* The first chapter is on a dialogue between the philosopher and the believer, the last one is on contemplative and discursive theology. The main body of the book analyzes the relationship between existential and doctrinal faith, and presents Christ as the foundation of faith. A modern reflective work steeped in scriptural traditions.

McShane, Philip, ed.
Foundations of Theology.
Dublin: Gill and Macmillan, 1971.
Language Truth and Meaning.
Dublin: Gill and Macmillan, 1972.

Theologians of stature from at home and abroad discourse on Lonergan's ideas, agree and disagree, compare them to others, or simply speak their minds on kindred subjects. All in all, learned conversations that, at some points, are an intellectual delight. The atmosphere is abstract and relaxed.

Muck, Otto.
The Transcendental Method.
New York: Herder and Herder, 1968.

A basic introduction to "transcendental Thomism." The better part of the book is given to explaining the theories of Maréchal. Shorter essays present the philosophical investigations of André Marc, Bernard Lonergan and Emerich Coreth.

Mussner, Franz.
Die Auferstehung Jesu.
Muenchen: Koesel, 1969.

This book is a model in showing how a new and richer understanding of an historical event can be achieved through the judicious application of hermeneutical principles.

Newman, John Henry Cardinal.
An Essay on the Development of Christian Doctrine.
Garden City, NY: Doubleday, Image Books, 1960.

> We like to think that if Newman were alive today he would give us a sequel to this book under the title "An Essay on the Development of the Capacity of the Christian Person to Understand the Mysteries." It would be another classic, as suited to our times as this first volume was suited to his times.

Palmer, Richard E.
Hermeneutics.
Evanston: Northwestern University Press, 1969.

> A survey of some modern interpretation theories. We found the author's "Thirty Theses on Interpretation" instructive and thought-provoking, even if not always agreed with.

Pannenberg, Wolfhart, *et al.*
History and Hermeneutic.
New York: Harper & Row, 1967.

> Seven outstanding authors from Germany write on the application of hermeneutical principles to history—religious and secular. A fine introduction into the realization of the complexity of issues and the diversity of opinions.

Teilhard de Chardin, Pierre.
The Phenomenon of Man.
New York: Harper & Row, 1961.

> We list this book to indicate that the knowledge of

Teilhard's thought is indispensable for any theological discourse on the development of man.

Tracy, David.
Blessed Rage for Order.
New York: Seabury, 1975.

The questions Tracy raises may well stay with us longer than some of the answers he reaches; that is often the way with brilliant researchers.

van Riet, Georges.
L'épistémologie thomiste. Recherches sur le problème de la connaissance dans l'Ecole Thomiste contemporaine.
Second edition.
Louvain: Nauwelaerts, 1950.
Problèmes d'épistémologie.
Louvain: Nauwelaerts, 1960.

These two books, one a systematic treatise, the other a collection of essays, are probably the best available introductions into the epistemological problem as it has been discussed by Catholic thinkers in modern times.

Voegelin, Eric.
Anamnesis.
Notre Dame: University of Notre Dame Press, 1978.

A philosophy of history, not directly concerned with theology. However, the reading of it is bound to provoke good questions concerning the historicity of the Church, its relationship to cultural trends and to the larger human community.

Some short studies that can serve as introductions into the study of the sacrament of penance at the Council of Trent. They contain abundant bibliography to help further research:

Berguecio, Julio Jimenez.
La penitencia: sacramento constitutivamente jurisdiccional.
Santiago: Universidad Catolica de Chile, 1975.

Braekmans, Ludwig.
Confession et communion au moyen age et au concile de Trente.
Paris: Desclée de Brouwer, 1971.

Fransen, Piet.
"Réflexions sur l'anathème au Concile de Trente."
Ephemerides Theologicae Lovanienses 29 (1953) 657-72.

Lennerz, Heinrich.
"Das Konzil von Trient und theologische Schulmeinungen"
Scholastik 4 (1929) 38-53.

————.

"Notulae Tridentinae, Primum Anathema in Concilio Tridentino."
Gregorianum 27 (1946) 136-42.

Peter, Carl.
"Auricular Confession and the Council of Trent."
The Jurist 28 (1968) 280-97.

All English translations of the Bible have been taken from: *The Oxford Annotated Bible with the Apocrypha,* Revised Standard Version. New York: Oxford University Press, 1965.

All English translations of the *New Rite of Penance* have been taken from: *The Rites of the Catholic Church.* English translation prepared by The International Commission on English in the Liturgy. New York: Pueblo Publishing Co., 1976.

All English translations of Vatican Council II documents have been taken from: Abbott, Walter M., ed. *The Documents of Vatican II.* New York: Guild Press, 1966.